I0069262

FINANCIAL FREEDOM THE ROYAL WAY

7 Commandments From the Networking Queen of Real Estate

Brooke Shang

10-10-10
Publishing

Financial Freedom the Royal Way
www.brookeshang.com
Copyright © 2020 Brooke Shang

ISBN: 978-1-77277-389-7

All rights reserved. No portion of this book may be reproduced mechanically, electronically, or by any other means, including photocopying, without permission of the publisher or author except in the case of brief quotations embodied in critical articles and reviews. It is illegal to copy this book, post it to a website, or distribute it by any other means without permission from the publisher or author.

Limits of Liability and Disclaimer of Warranty
The author and publisher shall not be liable for your misuse of the enclosed material. This book is strictly for informational and educational purposes only.

Warning – Disclaimer
The purpose of this book is to educate and entertain. The author and/or publisher do not guarantee that anyone following these techniques, suggestions, tips, ideas, or strategies will become successful. The author and/or publisher shall have neither liability nor responsibility to anyone with respect to any loss or damage caused, or alleged to be caused, directly or indirectly by the information contained in this book.

Publisher
10-10-10 Publishing
Markham, ON
Canada

Printed in Canada and the United States of America

GENERAL DISCLOSURE(S)

The information provided in this book is not designed or intended to qualify readers for employment. It is intended solely for the avocation, personal enrichment, and enjoyment of readers. The examples, (including but not limited to deals, spreadsheets, and additional tools and materials), are for educational and/or illustration purposes only, and are provided with the understanding that the author is not engaged in rendering legal, investment, accounting, or other professional advice.

Please note that investing involves risks. Any decision to invest in either the real estate or stock markets is a personal decision that should be made after thorough research, including an assessment of your personal risk tolerance and your personal financial condition and goals. Results are based on market conditions and on each individual and the action they take and the time and effort they put in. The education we provide and the strategies we teach are not intended to be a way to "get rich quick." The information contained in the following presentation is for educational and informational purposes only and should not be construed as legal advice or as being applicable to any person's specific situation. This presentation contains general information, concepts and strategies and may not reflect current legal developments or information.

LEGAL DISCLOSURE(S)

In some jurisdictions, licensing may be required to execute certain investing strategies and techniques that we teach. Discuss licensing and other regulatory requirements with your power team attorney to be sure you are in compliance with the jurisdictions in which you operate.

CONTRACTS, FORMS AND LETTERS DISCLOSURE(S)

All contracts, forms and letters contained herein are provided for training purposes only. The provider does not assert any warranty, express or implied, as to the legal effect and/or completeness of the contract, forms and letters. The provider hereby disclaims any and all liability with respect to their forms. The provider suggests that you contact an attorney to ensure that the contracts, forms and letters are modified to meet the laws of your state or province.

Under some circumstances you may require a license to perform certain wholesale strategies. Discuss with your power team attorney to determine any licensing requirements in your state or province.

Table of Contents

This book is dedicated to:

Future or current real estate investors with the curiosity to learn, and the entrepreneurial spirit to always do more, be more, and explore more opportunities.

Testimonials

The eagerness to learn and to act, combined with a passion to create a positive experience for anyone who encounters her, has made Brooke one of the most successful (yet extremely grounded) investors I've met. With a strong entrepreneurial spirit and business mindset, Brooke is someone who is intelligent, professional, and simply a pleasure to work with. She's a lady of her words, and her determination to make a difference for people in her life, including herself, are two great things that I admire about her the most.

Tim Tsai, International Award Winning Mentor, Founder & Principal, Trust Your Talent Academy, Edmonton AB

Trying to grow my real estate portfolio has been important to me. Brooke has been there since the beginning and, most importantly, has provided many opportunities for further returns. The duplex we worked on together generated double digit returns and collected top rents in the area. Doesn't matter what it has been, Brooke always gets it done! Never have to worry about excuses or problems with getting things done with her; she's very solution oriented.

Devin Duchesne, Owner of Maple Mountain Properties, Kirkland Lake, ON

No one knows RTO (Rent-to-Own) better than Brooke. Currently, Brooke has helped me generate more than $3000 per month in passive income as her joint venture partner. We continue to work on more deals together. I thank Brooke for everything that I have achieved today as a real estate investor. She has helped me open my mind to creative ways of investing. She has the patience of a mother and is able to stay calm and analyze the deals for what they are. She will assist you to stay focused, and she will open your mind to not let little things bog you down. Brooke has helped me grow, not only as an investor but as an individual.

Brooke's appreciative and helpful nature has put her ahead of her peers, and she is on her way to bigger and greater success. I'm very fortunate to ride the journey with her. I look forward to working together closely with Brooke for many years to come. Let's make a difference and also give back soon one day!!

George Wu, Real Estate Investor, High Net-worth Associate Investment Advisor, TD Bank, Richmond BC

With one rent to own deal, Brooke helped me generate more than $1,000 per month of cash flow as an investor. I would like to thank Brooke for being an honest and easy to work with business partner. Brooke is very thorough and also was quick to respond to any questions I asked. I look forward to growing my real estate portfolio by investing more money with Brooke in joint ventures.

Innocent Munyanyi, Real Estate Investor, Financial Service Advisor, Kitchener, ON

I count my blessings to have met Brooke and to have the opportunity to continue to collaborate with her. Anyone who gets the chance to work with her need not hesitate! I have had the pleasure to work with several JVs over the past year and, as a new investor, it is important to me that I work with JVs that are supportive and knowledgeable, and that understand the real estate business. Brooke possesses all these qualities and so much more, and has quickly become one of my go-to experts. I feel confident that when she structures a deal, it has been vetted and it is solid. She is caring and giving of her time.

Together, we are able to enjoy $1,200 of monthly cash flow and double digit ROI (return on investment) when we help the tenants to become homeowners at the rent-to-own program. I always look forward to talking and working with her. If you are in a position to work with Brooke on a deal, go for it; you will gain and learn so much from her!!

Rhondi Kablak, Real Estate Investor, Project Manager, Dynamic Attractions Ltd, Vancouver BC

Our rent-to-own deal generates $1,500 monthly cash flow and double digit ROI once tenants become homeowners. Brooke has been a constant source of inspiration since the beginning of my real estate investment journey. She is a true champion of the win-win, or go-giver mindset, which causes like-minded people to gravitate towards her.

With her family, career, coaching, and investing obligations, I am constantly amazed by her ability to demonstrate grace under pressure and time management skills.

Wayne Lee, Founder of W&E Homes Inc. Richmond BC

I had a really positive experience as Brooke's tenant. She is a great partner as a landlord—not only responsive but committed to quality solutions when investment is necessary. It is clear that she respects her property and is diligent and fair-minded in fulfilling landlord responsibilities. Highly recommended.

Cathleen Colehour, Past Tenant, Co-founder of the WILL DO Project, Toronto ON

Foreword

Are you on a journey of entrepreneurship or real estate investing, and searching for guidance on how to be successful and achieve your goals? *Financial Freedom the Royal Way* is based on seven simple principles that are duplicable and applicable. This book will equip you well for your journey in real estate investing.

The eagerness to learn and to act, combined with a passion to make an impact on tenants, students and investors, have made Brooke Shang a successful real estate investor. With a strong work ethic and entrepreneurial mindset, she is intelligent, professional, and simply a pleasure to work with. It is hard to imagine that only a few years ago, Brooke was a stay-at-home mom without any streams of income. With financial education, she took action and was able to achieve financial freedom in three years. Brooke made it look easy, living her life the royal way and doing it all. Now she is traveling, writing, balancing a family life, working as a management consultant in the corporate world, investing, and teaching about real estate with multiple streams of income.

Brooke's experience and stories show that you can always do more and be more. Whether you think you are too old to start, too busy to learn, or too poor to invest, there are no excuses. Don't let this book be another dust collector on your bookshelf. Let it inspire and prepare you to get out of your comfort zone and take action. The book is designed to open your mind to creative investing strategies, and overcome obstacles and negative self-talk. It will give you the tools, the mindset and the knowledge that will serve you on your real estate investment journey, if you choose to take action and apply what you learn.

Whether you are new or already investing, I applaud your effort to learn through Brooke Shang's example. You too can live the life of your dreams. The fact that you are reading this book means you are on the right track to bettering yourself and experience *Financial Freedom the Royal Way.*

Raymond Aaron
New York Times Bestselling Author

Acknowledgements

Whatever I have achieved in my life, I owe it all to my relationships and the wonderful people I have encountered in my life, who have made me who I am today. Thank you for injecting positive energy into my life. At the risk of forgetting some names, I would like to thank some of those who made financial freedom possible for me.

I would like to first thank my husband, **Doug Berry**, for believing in me, supporting me, and taking on more at home so that I could pursue my dreams. Most importantly, thank you for letting me be me. I know I can always trust and count on you to be there for me. I really appreciate the fact that you are getting out of your comfort zone for me to sign on the dotted lines, and taking on huge debt or mortgages to build our real estate empire, for the sake of our kids too.

I would like to thank my beautiful babies, **Donny and Chelsea**, for being my WHY, for my unlimited hugs and kisses, and for teaching me to see the world from a different angle. I consider myself unbelievably lucky to have you in my life. I thank the Universe every day for entrusting your lives in our hands. You are the best kids, even though you always tell me that I am partial. In addition, thank you, **Donny,** for being my accountability partner in writing. I love it when we do something together.

My dad, **Chi-Hsin Shang**, passed away in 2017, but the legacy lives on. Dad, you were the calm and quiet listener, but whenever you opened your mouth, you always had a presence, and always had something profound and intelligent to say. Therefore, growing up, I learned that if you do not have anything brilliant to say, shut up! Everybody knew you as the most gentle, generous, and kind soul. I do not remember, not even once, you raising your voice at us. We were by no means the perfect kids. I happen to be writing this paragraph on Father's Day. I feel like I am on the path you were on before, being an author, an entrepreneur, and now an educator. I often reflected on what you would do, Dad, in different circumstances. We have grown up to be provided with the best opportunities and resources you and mom could give us. I can honestly say that we still benefit from our upbringings today. I still talk to you in my head a lot, because you are still guiding me throughout my journey.

My mom, **Gloria Shang**, the one that gave me life and exemplified what it is like to be a parent. You are an extraordinary chef and a very talented painter. We are so blessed to grow up with gourmet and healthy meals. Thank you for raising me to be who I am today. I never believed that there was any limitation for being short, being a girl, or being an immigrant in Canada. I know that being me is enough, and actually more than enough. Most importantly, being a parent myself, and growing up in a loving environment, I have the comfort of knowing that no matter what I do, you would always be supportive and proud of me.

I have to thank my sister, **Lisa Shang,** for being the biggest influence for me growing up. We should always feel lucky to have funny people in our lives to make us laugh or fall off our chairs. Your unique humor makes people wonder how your brain is wired. You are the most optimistic person I have ever known. Thank you for bringing all the joy and fun into my life. Thank you for treating and loving my kids like your own. I know... they are perfect!!

Linda Berry, Ron Berry, and **Maria Berry,** for being the best in-laws ever. I know I am lucky to have your love and support. Thank you for letting us always just show up at your places with a phone call.

I am forever grateful to my mentor, **Tim Tsai**, and his partner, **Rey Salazar**. I would not be where I am on the investment journey if not for you as my mentor, my friend, and business partner. It is crazy how my life has been so different since we met. You led by example. I have not only learned about real estate investing, but about personal development as well. Thank you for also pushing me to be better, to grow, to live by example with integrity, and to truly care about the people we work with. In addition, thank you, **Tim**, for creating *"Trust Your Talent"* as the platform for quality real estate education, so that we can help more people reach financial freedom and financial independence. My peers on the *Trust Your Talent* team: **Gustavo, Jeffrey, Jon, Kyle, Liliam, Rolando, Ryan, Vince,** and **Chewy**. We are now family. Thank you all for making working together toward the same mission such a fun and rewarding experience.

Thank you, **Pip Stehlik**, for getting me started. I was in Pip's class on September 16th, 2016. I remember it like yesterday, because I kept thinking back to that day. My life started to change as a real estate investor. I had so much fun. I went in the class thinking, "I will be pitched. It's just another presentation." Instead, I was so entertained and inspired. The energy filled the room, and everybody could feel Pip's passion for the subject. I just thought I wanted to be like Pip. Even until this day, Pip continues to provide the support I need. When I look back and think how I would want to make an impact on other people's lives, I always look up to Pip. As an investor, or anybody who started on the journey of their dreams, you will always remember the first day and the first person that got you started.

George Wu, thank you for being the best friend a girl could have, and for trusting in me and going through ups and downs as my bestie/investor. Whatever problems we have encountered throughout our journey together, I know we can always work it out together.

Cathy Kim and **Tiffany Lin**, thank you for being my 20/30/40 ladies in the real estate community. I love the support and seeing each other's personal growth. Also, thank you, **Cathy**, for being so patient.

You always go the extra mile to help your clients out. Looking forward to many more deals together, my go-to realtor!

Thank you, **John Kuhn,** for being the most efficient human being I have ever known and make collaborative work interesting despite some difficult times in our professional careers.

I want to say thank you to my group of best friends since junior high, in no particular order: **Yuyu, Maruko, Candy, Daphne, Sidney, Samantha, Joanna,** and **Sarah Y.** Now our group has expanded to include **Chichi, Tina,** and **Caroline.** It is ridiculous how we have not stopped chatting since we were thirteen. We started by sending letters. We have gone through the ICQ age, Microsoft Messenger, and now several social media. We have been friends since we were thirteen.

Thank you, my baby gang mommy friends, **Hani, Sandhya, Carla, Dana**, **Marilu,** and **Ping,** for being such great and supportive friends since our babies were.... babies. I love how we have always exchanged mommy notes and found deals for each other.

Bob Burg, co-author of *The Go-Giver* book series, thank you for your kind message and encouragement. It means a lot from an author I look up to. Thank you for the simple yet powerful messages from the book. The five laws of stratospheric success: value, compensation, influence, authenticity, and receptivity are such simple reminders of how we should set our intentions to live our days by.

As Doug always says, "**Oprah (Winfrey)** does not live with us." I know, I sometimes speak as if Oprah just gave me an inspirational quote during our conversation. That is how powerful and down to earth Oprah's teaching is. **Oprah,** I know you do not know me YET. I am sending you a copy of my book, because the thought of being able to send you a copy after I am done was such a great motivator for me to finish the book. Whenever I need some guidance, or need to be inspired, I can just search a speech that Oprah did. Listen to or read *The*

Wisdom of Sundays for a quick read. I can randomly flip to a page to get motivated and see what message the Universe is sending me through the book. These are the quotes I came across while writing this paragraph:

"The number one principle that rules my life is intention. Thought by thought, choice by choice, we are co-creating our lives based on the energy of our intention." – **Oprah**

"My goal is to live my life as a more awakened, vibrant, alive human being. My prayer is to not let any moment pass without my acknowledgment and full experience of it. In order to do that, I've got to practice." – **Oprah**

We are all connected. Thank you for being part of my journey.

Introduction

Y ou might think a tool book is exactly what you need to get yourself started in real estate investing. It is important to be financially literate and to understand the science of money. Before you take the first step and start learning, in addition to learning about different real estate investing strategies along the way, the biggest part of a real estate investing journey is actually about growth mindset. I have always been interested in personal growth and development, and found the spiritual world fascinating. In Chinese, we call spiritual intelligence "root of wisdom." This term is used to describe people who can digest and absorb the knowledge they have obtained, with wisdom and clarity. There is nothing new under the sun. Hence, I have used many quotes throughout the book, from people with amazing "root of wisdom."

Readers want to be inspired and entertained, not preached to. This is something I have learned from the MasterClass on writing, and from the movie "Little Women." My intention is to take you through the journey and use real life stories and examples of my deals, to show you how it works. Everybody is unique in terms of interest, resources, personality types, and skill sets. My journey is unique to me, but the system is certainly duplicable to you. You can use one, or use hybrid strategies that suit you, once you are educated and take action to be the expert.

People often ask me a lot of technical questions on real estate investing. I am happy to help. That is what I love about the real estate community as well. People are willing to help, and they are generous in sharing knowledge and making recommendations. (Make your own educated judgement to decide what advice to take on.) However, people without the right mindsets and financial literacy often ask the wrong or unrelated questions. They are looking for answers to validate their limiting beliefs, and giving themselves more reasons to procrastinate. Often, that will not lead them anywhere; it keeps them exactly where they are in real estate investing, for years and years.

I am only sharing what I have learned and experienced so that you can overcome your self-doubts of having no time, no money, and no skills. These are just false notions of the obstacles. You do not have to reinvent the wheel or start from scratch. I also have doubts while I am writing this book, because there are people who are better writers than I am, or more experienced as real estate investors than I am. With so much on my plate, I wondered if I could really finish writing the book. However, it would be selfish of me not to share the valuable lessons I have learned. This is what kept me going on finishing the book. Everybody's journey is different. I feel blessed every day to be given the opportunities and be on the path I am on now. There are speed bumps along the way, of course. It is not meant to be easy. That is why there is only a small percentage of people taking on the challenge of being an entrepreneur or real estate investor. Nevertheless, it is not impossible; as you can see, there are people that have already done it before you.

I only ask you to keep an open mind. Every experience or every book you read is meant to be a learning opportunity.

Commandment 1

Finding the Whys

Why Am I Writing This Book?

I f you want a challenge and to hold yourself accountable, or if you would like to give back and share your knowledge, as those who came before you did, write a book. Everybody has something to offer. You may not know what it is yet. Let the wisdom channel through you. This is how I convinced myself to start writing this book.

> *"We write for the same reason that we walk, talk, climb mountains or swim the oceans— because we can. We have some impulse within us that makes us want to explain ourselves to other human beings. That's why we paint, that's why we dare to love someone—because we have the impulse to explain who we are."*
> **~ Maya Angelou**

If you have kids, it is never difficult to convince yourself to do anything, because you want to set an example for them and make an impact on their lives in any way possible. I am never the one to pass up any good opportunities presented to me. Now I have this opportunity to write a book. Besides the book, I was offered the opportunity to speak, coach, and teach before the New Year. The path is clear to me. This is the year I brand myself and give back with what I have learned and gained through my journey as a real estate investor in the past three years. I truly believe that life happens for you at the right time for the right reason, when you are ready. This may be the very reason you picked up my book and started reading. You are ready to take action and get on your path to financial freedom through real estate investments. Alternatively, you could be like my friends and family who are not into real estate investing, and are just curious about what I have to say. In that case, I really appreciate your support.

> *"Setting an example is not the main means*
> *of influencing others; it is the only means."*
> ~ **Albert Einstein**

I read, but I am a very slow reader. I have written reports, papers, and tests throughout my academic years. I would force myself to read boring textbooks if the information proved to be useful. This is not one of those tool books for the analytical type. Time is everything. I am not gifted with the ability to read and internalize information quickly, even though I enjoy being constantly inspired and enlightened by the wisdom that good books can provide. Therefore, I want you to enjoy your time reading my book. Knowing the way I read and absorb information and knowledge, my intention is to share my stories and experiences that have worked for me to reach financial freedom through real estate, in a way that you can relate. This is more about you than it is about me.

Why Are You Reading This Book?

You are ready to take action, and you want proof that reaching financial freedom through real estate investing is achievable, and that the process is duplicable. You, too, can have the time and resources to enjoy your time with loved ones like the royals.

You want to learn, and I can totally relate. Learning has always been a big part in my life. My parents are both educators, so I have gone through a lot of schooling. Because I was put through it, and my parents believed in education, I understand that the reason you are reading my story, or any other accomplished investor's story for that matter, is to validate that financial freedom or independence is achievable. By seeing other people not that different from you doing it, you know that you can do it too.

When I first started with real estate as my side hustle, I still worked as a management consultant, and still do at the time of writing this paragraph, while raising two beautiful kids with the support of my husband, Doug. Being a mom, being there for my kids' activities and spending quality time with them is still the most important role I have. For many people, financial freedom means not having a J.O.B. (just over broke) any more. There is nothing wrong with that if you hate your job, no longer feel fulfilled, and need to get out of it. To me, freedom means doing what you enjoy and having the ability to choose. I have the ability to replace my day job income already. Regardless, I am still able to work as a management consultant, so why not double my income?

To retain the knowledge and make it useful to you, you need to apply and take action. There is no other way. I have a couple of shining degrees. It adds value to people who believe in the credentials and the school system. It showed that I could do it, and that I did it. However, what good does it do if the information in the textbooks is not applicable or does not contribute to my success and growth as a person? What good does it do if you do not take action with the information you spent time to get and the knowledge you have obtained?

Taking action and achieving your goals requires some hard work. More importantly, it requires having the right mindset and a belief that is so strong that you can almost taste it and actually feel the excitement of success.

Success looks a lot like hard work. Think back to a situation where you achieved your goals or felt that you had succeeded. What did you feel or experience while working toward your goal or goals? What is your list?

	SUCCESS	
Failure	Objection handling	What is your list?
Vision	Late nights	———————
Courage	Naysayers	———————
Action	Dreams	———————
Self-doubt	Dedication	———————

> *"Whether you think you can or think you can't,*
> *either way you are right."*
> ~ Henry Ford

You probably hear this a lot as well: I believe that if I can do it, you can do it too.

The 10-secound barrier: It is the physical and psychological barrier to complete a 100-metre sprint in under 10 seconds. Since the first person, Jim Hines, did it in the late 1960s, there have been more and more athletes able to break the barrier. When somebody shows you that it can be done, you will be able to achieve what used to be perceived as the impossible.

Why Did I Start Real Estate Investing?

My husband, Doug, and I were always responsible with our finances. We have always contributed to RRSPs, never had a balance on our credit cards, had a mortgage with very low LTV (Loan to Value), and had a Camry we bought outright; and even leasing our second car made us quite nervous about having a monthly payment.

I have read many of Robert Kiyosaki's books. I thought the idea was fantastic. However, I did not know exactly how to be a "Rich Dad." Instead, I watched the Suze Orman show on TV. I read *The Wealthy Barber* and *The Automatic Millionaire*. We followed their teaching of saving as much as we could, living below our means and praying that we would be "fine" by the time we retire. If you have the discipline to save and constantly live below your means, go for it! However, we did not find it easy if we wanted to live the royal way. We have families abroad. We enjoy eating out and traveling.

At the time, we saved and did not really splurge on anything. I admit there is a sense of accomplishment when you can get things cheaper than most people can. There is nothing wrong with that. This is great when you are a wholesaler, and you should always find money in the buy, in a real estate deal.

My checkbox life might seem to be what people consider as the dream life, in a conventional way. Here is what I mean by "checkbox." I went to good schools, got good grades, and never had boy problems. Like a stereotype good Asian kid, I completed my MBA and found a corporate job. I got married, had two beautiful kids, and contributed to RRSPs. It sounds like the kind of life most people are pursuing, doesn't it? I checked all the boxes of being a good person and having a stable life. However, we all need variety in life. See the next page for an illustration of what a checkbox life would look like.

☑ Get good grades in school
☑ Hang out with the good kids
☑ No boy/girl troubles
☑ No drugs, No partying
☑ Get into good schools
☑ Complete graduate school
☑ Find a corporate job
☑ Get married
☑ Have kids
☑ Work
☑ Retire

"If you are always trying to be normal,
you will never know how amazing you can be."
~ **Maya Angelou**

Nevertheless, to live like this, it felt like we were always on a "financial diet." When my father retired and his health started to deteriorate, I realized that you *do not* spend less after you retire. The cost of private rooms, and new drugs not covered by health care, certainly added up quickly. Even if you are healthy, you want to see the world or take your grandkids to Disney World. Whoever said you would spend less after you retire is not being realistic. People who follow this path are just too afraid to expect more in life.

I finally took action and decided I had to do something if we wanted to be more than just comfortable. I believe "life happens for you," at the right time and the right place, for the right reason, when you are ready to be at the next level in life. In September 2016, I attended a real estate investing weekend workshop. I saw the ad on Facebook and decided that we had been on a "financial diet" long enough. "If somebody is willing to show me how, I am willing to take the chance and invest in the education," I thought.

I am learning every day, and constantly getting out of my comfort zone as a professional real estate investor. I know I am trained and ready for the next level.

Again, find a strong "why." Studies have shown that even the most persistent and hardworking people can get burnt out, lose momentum, or even completely lose interest in what they are doing if they do not know "why" they are doing it.

Did I give you enough reasons why you can do it too?

I hope my experience resonates with you as an immigrant, as a parent, as somebody who is still working, or as a real estate investor.

Find Your Why, Set Goals and Take Action

"You don't have to be great to start,
but you have to start to be great."
~ Zig Ziglar

Don't overthink it. Don't wait till the perfect moment or the perfect circumstances to start. Are you still waiting for the perfect opportunity? All those people waiting for a market correction to buy real estate are still waiting for the right moment to take action. The more you overthink, the more you procrastinate. The best time to start is now. Even if you just take one step at a time, it will add up to something. Once you see the progress, even if just a little bit at a time, you will be motivated to do more and take the next step. Don't wait for "someday." Let today be "Day 1."

"The journey of a thousand miles begins with one step."
~ Lao Tzu

Taking action does not mean you are going to accomplish everything right away, or give yourself the pressure to be an overachiever, although it does not hurt. Taking action means improving and getting better, one step at a time. Most people overestimate what they can achieve in a year, and underestimate what they can achieve in ten years.

I have gone through my whys, and why you should read this book. In terms of real estate, why are you getting into investment? Remember, real estate is not just about brick and mortar. You are looking for an emotionally-charged WHY to get you through the inevitable challenges you will encounter throughout your journey, so that you will not quit. You will keep the momentum going and persistently take action. You are responsible for your own success. In the next chapter, I will teach you how to train yourself to have the right mindset.

To help you get started, go through the "Finding Your Why Exercise" first. Keep an open mind as you continue to read....

Finding Your Why Exercise

What is your "why?" Here are some questions to guide you and help you find out what your "why" is.

1. Why do I want to invest in real estate?

    *   Legacy for my family
    *   Secured retirement
    *   Financial freedom
    *   Extra income to afford an extra vacation every year

2. What gets me out of bed excited every morning is:

    _____

3. I feel happy when I:

    _____

4. When I reach my real estate investment, and if money is no object, my purpose in life is:

    _____

5. Live every day like it is the last day of your life. If I knew I only had a few days to live, I would:

    _____

As I am writing this section, my kids are sitting right next to me on either side. If you have kids, you know that it is a no-brainer that your kids are your "why." We are lucky to witness the miracle of life, to have such pure and amazing souls in our lives, and to learn what giving and unconditional love is all about. I am looking at their cute faces, thinking that they deserve the best I can provide them. Of course, we are not perfect. Besides providing them the best life we can afford, we are also setting examples as parents, and as investors, of who we are and how we do things. With this in mind, it is easy to constantly remind ourselves to do the right thing, be ethical, and do what we promised ourselves we would do. The funny thing is that my kids would use my words against me when making an argument.

"Don't add time." (Do it now, Mommy.)

"It is more important to be kind than to be right." (Mommy, can I be right this time?)

Set Your Goals

Now that you have gone through the exercise to find your "why," the next step is to set your goals. When you define your goals, you give your brain something to look for and to focus your energy on. Successful people clearly know what their goals are. They know who they are and what they want in life. They write it down, and they make plans for its accomplishments.

"Direction determines destination.
Set a goal for what it will make of you to achieve.
The greatest value in life is not what you get;
it is what you become. What will this
make of you in the process?"
~ Jim Rohn

S.M.A.R.T. goal setting could be a common and easy way to remember to start your goal setting. It stands for: (S) specific, (M) measurable, (A) attainable, (R) realistic, and (T) time bound. Follow the S.M.A.R.T. acronym. Ensure that you give yourself a deadline to achieve it. We all like things simple and effective.

There are a lot of good books on finding your "why" and goal setting, such as **Start with Why**, by Simon Sinek.

Your goals might change throughout the course, but your "why" will stay the same.

Here are some examples:

<u>Why</u>	<u>Goals</u>
Improve standard of living for the family	*Stage 1:* Have enough passive income to cover the mortgage or rent
	Stage 2: An extra family trip per year
	Stage 3: Cover all living expenses

When you write down your goals, ask yourself these questions:

1. Is what I am doing today, getting me closer to where I want to be tomorrow?

_____

2. Is this the direction I want in my life, or somebody else's direction? Is it mine?

_____

"If your success is defined by the traditions, then you are destined to be unhappy, because you have no control over it."
~ Jeff Weiner

3. What am I doing that works, and what am I doing that does not work?

_____

"The secret to unleashing your true power is setting goals that are exciting enough that they truly inspire your creativity and ignite your passion."
~ Tony Robbins

In the first couple of years of my investing journey, I did not set my goals high enough. It was a learning process. There were a lot of opportunities. My goal was just to prove to myself that it could work, and any extra income would help. There is nothing wrong with that. Sometimes I wonder though if I could have achieved more as a real estate investor if I dared to dream bigger. I only took on smaller deals when I started. Nevertheless, I took action.

"Do not set your goals too low.
If your dreams do not scare you, they are not big enough."
~Ellen Johnson Sirleaf

This year I have set a few goals for myself. I am willing to share as an example. I wrote down these goals for this year:

1. Move to a single-detached home in the school district (We are currently in a semi.)
2. Be an inspiring and amazing speaker
3. Finish my book (If you have this book in hand, I have reached my goal. Time to celebrate!! J)
4. Financial goals: 5 rent-to-own deals; increase cash flow by 30%; increase our net worth by half a million

Write down your goals. Decide what your goals are and write down your list of goals.

_____

_____

_____

Here is a statement you could use:

I, _____, commit to complete these goals by (date).

When I achieve these goals, my life will improve in the following way: (This usually circles back to your why.)

I will reward myself with _____

Signed: _____

Date: _____

Commandment 3

Be Your Own Teacher

&

Train Yourself to Get Out of the Comfort Zone

You are your own teacher. You are the one getting things done. You might feel that you are just getting paid enough not to quit, and you are doing just enough not to get fired. If that is the case, it is time to get out of your comfort zone. I can honestly say that I am never in the comfort zone anymore, but I am constantly learning and growing. It takes courage to quit your day job. It takes courage to start a business. It takes courage to pivot. Nevertheless, it is worth it, and it is all about having the courage to get out of your comfort zone.

I have people asking me what my easiest deal was. Sometimes things just happen. My easiest deal was when I was about to take on a deal while I was away for a business trip in Dallas, Texas. Since I was away and occupied during my business trip, timing was not the best. However, all I did was just connect an investor with somebody, with the deal I was going to take on, and I received about $1,000 as a referral fee. It took me a matter of minutes. However, I cannot always expect to get a deal done in a matter of minutes, and this is definitely not my most memorable deal, because I did not have to get out of my comfort zone. Why don't you ask me what my most memorable deal was? Nonetheless, I validated that yes, your network is your network.

Join groups, and connect with like-minded people. These may be the people outside of your usual circle. The trick is getting comfortable with being uncomfortable. Putting myself out there was the most uncomfortable thing I had to do. Even though some people may know me as the Networking Queen of Real Estate (hence, **Financial Freedom the "Royal Way"**), it was actually very uncomfortable for me to go to different networking events and then meet strangers in the real estate community. Now I have an amazing network and am constantly referring my power team to investors. It paid off. Often, things just happen organically due to the network I have built.

To reach the next level, I have started to teach, coach, and have speaking engagements. It is also very uncomfortable for me to write about my own experience. Since my MBA class, I have not really had to do any public speaking. Even at my corporate job, all I had to do was reporting when I present. It is very different from having to really write a speech or decide what to say to keep the audience engaged. I was so bad that I could literally hear my voice shake. I have since improved, and continue to learn to be a great speaker and to get over my own fear. I have gradually stopped doubting myself before I speak.

"A person's success in life can usually be measured
by the number of uncomfortable conversations
he or she is willing to have."
~ Tim Ferriss, author of *The 4-Hour Workweek*

The first thing you will encounter when you step out of the comfort zone will be fear.

The best thing in life is on the other side of fear. Counter fear with the size of your dreams.

> *"Inaction breeds doubt and fear.*
> *Action breeds confidence and courage.*
> *If you want to conquer fear,*
> *do not sit home and think about it.*
> *Go out and get busy."*
> **~ Dale Carnegie**

Make sure you have completed the "Finding Your Why Exercise." Commit to your own success and a strong enough WHY that you are passionate about. When problems arise, the problems are not so bad that you will change your mind in persuading your dreams. Having a strong "why" will make all the excuses seem weak. Believe in yourself that you can do it. You can sense how liberating reaching financial freedom is, just by thinking about it. If you are not taking action to get out of your comfort zone, you are too comfortable being unsuccessful.

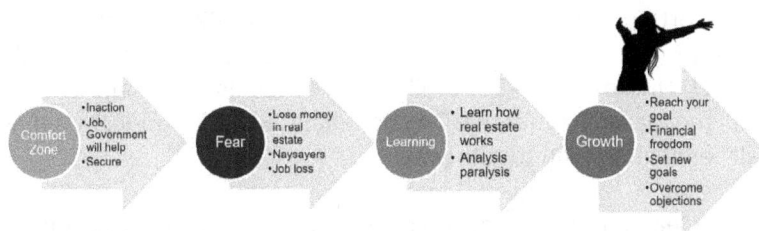

> *"You never change your life until you step out of your comfort*
> *zone; change begins at the end of your comfort zone."*
> **~ Roy T. Bennett**

As you probably noticed as well, when you do try to stay in your comfort zone, you are never truly comfortable. There is always a natural desire in you to want more and a better life than the one you have now. The more comfortable you are today, the more uncomfortable you will be in the future. There is no such thing as job security any more. To find an easy way out, I have heard people saying, "If I cannot find a job, I will just work at McDonald's." Nowadays, even McDonald's is not hiring as many people, since customers are now using apps and touch screen menus at the restaurants. I have also had good tenants who lost their jobs all of a sudden and could not pay rent anymore. Even if you still have a very comfortable job right now, you might just happen to be in the right industry at the right time at the moment. It could happen to you too. Most of the companies operating today will not be around in 10 years. Ninety-six percent of businesses fail within 10 years, according to INC.com. Nevertheless, there is no reason to be upset or discouraged about this fact, or to give up your dreams to be an investor. You are reading this book and getting out of your comfort zone. You are already ahead of 90% of the people staying in their comfort zone.

The first step to get out of your comfort zone is always the hardest, but change is the only constant. Even if you want to stay inside your little bubble and stay in your comfort zone, you might not have that choice. By the time you retire, the government may not have enough to support you or help you at retirement. For 2020, the maximum monthly benefit is **$1,175.83**—but the average monthly benefit is only **$672.87**. Unlike CPP, OAS is available to all Canadians at age 65. For 2020, the maximum monthly OAS benefit is **$613.53**. Seriously, is that really enough for you to retire on?

The fear and the realization may finally prompt you to get out of your comfort zone. In Taiwan, where I grew up, retirees in the public sectors used to be able to receive 18% interest with their savings. Not too long ago, this benefit was taken away. Public sector retirees can no longer depend on the high interest rates, and their pensions were also reduced significantly. There is a lot of political discussion around the subject, which I do not intend to get into. The point is "control." We have no control over the government spending, or how the policies will change by the time we retire. As professional real estate investors, we get educated and gain financial literacy to gain control. We are not speculators.

> *"Risk comes from not knowing what you are doing."*
> **~ Warren Buffet**

Getting educated is key to getting to the next level. The process of applying the knowledge, and taking action to reach your goals, is where you will experience growth. Once you are there and comfortable, get uncomfortable again and set another goal for growth.

> *"Focus on where you want to go, not on what you fear."*
> **~ Tony Robbins**

When I got my first rent-to-own deal, I certainly felt the fear, and I was doubting myself as to whether I could actually get the deal done. Quoting Tony Robbins again, I should have focused on where I wanted to go, not on the fear. I had already taken the class on the subject. However, it was quite overwhelming when it came to actually applying the knowledge. The fear came from my inexperience. I wholesaled the deal to a fellow investor. We remain good friends today, and do more deals together. In this case, "wholesale" simply means that I passed the deal on to another investor for a fee. I did not know him before he approached me for this deal, even though we have the same mentor. We had a mutual connection, and I did check if this investor was easy to work with and could actually qualify to get the deal done. Again, your network is your net worth. It is important to have somebody you trust to give you referrals or input.

When I first met the tenant, he came in with a stash of cash. He told me he was in contraction, and that it was common for him to carry cash for transactions. It was certainly not something I was used to. I had my mentor on the phone while signing the documents with the tenant, buyers, and my investor, at a Tim Horton's after the inspection was done. I remember that the tenant's eyes turned red, and he looked like he was about to punch somebody when we could not agree on a few terms. It took us hours, and we were there until almost midnight. Rent-to-own or lease option is a more advanced strategy, which I will discuss further in later chapters. Being new at this at the time, there were a few terms I was not clear on when I communicated with the tenant. I feared that the tenant would back out. I feared that the investor was so firm on a few terms that he would actually walk away from it. I was afraid that I might not complete this deal that I had worked so hard on.

Fortunately, I had my mentor, and my investor had done a few rent-to-own deals before he took on my first rent-to-own deal. We were trained and educated the same way. It is a lot easier to work with people with the same education and mindset. He was firm on his terms, and the tenant eventually agreed. It was a great learning opportunity for me.

This was just the beginning. I got out of my comfort zone and faced fear. Rent-to-own was the strategy I focused on, and it eventually helped me reach my goal of having the cash flow to replace my working income. After doing so many deals, I still have doubts and fear when I go through the process. I am constantly uncomfortable. Nevertheless, the end results are always rewarding.

Exercise: "Comfort Zone Model"

1. **Comfort Zone:** Think of a situation where you feel stuck. Everything seems to be good or fine in life, but you feel life is dull.

   _____

2. **Fear:** Refer to your answer to the last question. What is your fear? Why do you want to get out of your current comfort zone?

   _____

3. **Learn:** What can you learn, and what knowledge do you need to apply to overcome your fear?

   _____

4. **Growth:** Time to celebrate! What will or have you been able to achieve?

   _____

   Take it a step further and think how you can get out of the comfort zone again and get yourself to the next level.

Train Yourself to Find the "How": No Excuses

"The only thing standing between you and your dream
is the bullshit story you keep telling yourself
as to why you cannot achieve it."
~ Jordan Belfort

You might think you are too busy to start investing. You are probably tired, overworked, and sick. You have kids, and you are still working full time. When your kid is sick, you have to drop everything you are doing to take care of your baby. I get that. After all, a high-stake game, such as real estate investing, requires a lot of your time, attention, and resources. These are the disempowering stories you are telling yourself so that you will not take action. If you do not take the leap of faith, it is impossible to fail at something you never do. On the other hand, there is no chance of winning either, if you do not participate. You can spend all day complaining how everything seems impossible, or all day doing what you know you are supposed to do. The choice is yours.

"It always seems impossible until it's done."
~ Nelson Mandela

I came to Canada when I was in high school, and I completed grade 12 and OAC. (Yes, back in the days, there was OAC if you wanted to get into universities.) Being an ESL student just taught me how to ace exams, being that I was a slow reader and only understood 60% of what the teachers said in class. I still got through, all the way to graduate school, and received an MBA from a top Canadian business school. I never would have thought I would be publishing a book in English. I do not mean to brag. My intention is to make a point here. No excuses.

> ***"He that is good for making excuses is***
> ***seldom good for anything else."***
> **~ Benjamin Franklin**

I had been a stay-at-home mom since I was married, until my oldest, Donny, was nine years old, and my youngest, Chelsea, just started full-day kindergarten. I thoroughly enjoyed my time being with the kids during those years. It is a dream of many parents not to miss any previous moments. I am extremely fortunate to be able to be there for them. In addition, I do think kids benefit from having their parents' attention at a young age. Being away from the job market for ten years, I did not expect to have a career and get back to the corporate world. Neither could I imagine balancing work and family life—taking the little monsters around to their activities and birthday parties. If you have been a full-time parent, you know that your brain is trained to see your kids as the center of your Universe. With so much on the go, you just cannot imagine having time to do anything else.

Are kids your excuses not to have time to do anything in life? If you want to do something that you love or believe in, I am sure you will find the time to do it. I have seen quite a few parents taking their babies to the Toronto Raptor's game, cheering at 10 o'clock at night. They just put noise-canceling headphones on the babies and have a great time. It is a very cute scene when you think about it. If something is important to you, such as a date night, you will find somebody to babysit. You can listen to a podcast on real estate while you are driving, or read a chapter whenever you can. Educating yourself is important. It adds up. Speaking of which, here is a book I would recommend: *The Compound Effect*, by Darren Hardy. Do a little bit at a time. It adds up.

Your kids should not be your distraction. They should be your "why." With the technologies these days, you can read and listen to podcasts any time. You can listen to an audiobook while you are waiting for your kids, when they are taking swimming lessons or during a birthday party. Side note: Birthday parties are the best. Somebody is entertaining your kids. Kids are having fun and spending time with their friends while you get a couple of hours off.

You are never too busy to do a little bit at a time. No excuses.

> ***"If it is important to you, you will find a way.***
> ***If not, you will find an excuse."***
> **~ Jim Rohn**

I got back into the workforce because I reconnected with an ex-colleague from Taiwan, who was coming to Toronto for a business trip. I saw his post on Facebook that he was in town, and I was just excited see somebody from my past life. Again, your network is your net worth. It turned out that he was in town to visit local vendors, and since I knew the business, I could be the liaison between the third party in Canada and his company in the States. The rest was history.

I knew I had degrees, but that was it. Being out of the labor force for so long, I honestly did not think that I had any employable skills. I remember, when I went back to work, my biggest concerns were that I would not remember how to use Excel, and learning the new systems. I was in my late 30s, and I was not confident that I could learn anything quickly. I almost did not take the job because of Excel. Looking back, this was such a BS excuse to do nothing, so that I could never fail.

> ***"Be a spectator of your own thoughts."***
> **~ Ray Chambers**

When self-doubts and negative thoughts arise, be mindful and be a spectator of your own thoughts. Do not let excuses stop you. List some excuses that are holding you back. Whenever you hear excuses in your head, remind yourself that it is just a thought. It is just an excuse (e.g., not smart enough, not strong enough, no money, no time, no talent, no experience, wrong upbringing….).

List of Excuses	What will you do?
E.g., I have no money.	Learn to spot opportunities. Learn to find $.
_____	_____
_____	_____
_____	_____
_____	_____

Let Failure Be Your Best Teacher

Be comfortable with failing, so that it is not a concern in your life. No experience should ever be wasted unless you let it be. From my experience, this requires you to always be mindful of all the lessons life is bringing to you. Draw inspiration from it and embrace change. Failure humbles you. I am often asked about any deals that have gone wrong. If you have done enough deals, something must have gone wrong before. It is not a matter of if; it is a matter of when. I do not think you ask me this question to discredit me. You might want to challenge me that real estate investing is not always as great as I claim it to be. Or you want to make sure that you will be okay even when things go wrong. Even with challenges, it is still worth it when you reach your financial freedom. Instead, it validates that it is okay to fail.

"I never lose. I win or I learn."
~ Nelson Mandela

Failure is just success in disguise. My biggest loss so far was the second deal I had done since I started learning about real estate. At the time, I just wanted to do a deal. Stock traders sometimes call it itchy fingers, meaning that you just want to do something. The money is there. You have the urge to just do something. It happens more often in stock trading, because a transaction is only a click away. There is no buyer's remorse. In real estate investing, there is usually a conditional period, and at least a month or so before closing. However, at the time, I really just wanted to get in a deal, and the investment was affordable. I made the mistake of not consulting my mentor, because I wanted to invest regardless.... Itchy fingers. If I had consulted my mentor, it would have been a $50,000 mistake that I could have avoided. It was a 23-unit, multi-family building. I did not invest my last dollar, so I thought it was worth it, even as a learning opportunity. The mistake I made was that I trusted the working partner too easily before I did my due diligence. He was not experienced enough to take on such a big project. It was not a strategy or a market I was familiar with.

Investing is about control. I did not have control over the project. As investors and limited partners, we would not see the return until the project was completed and refinanced. We really did not have much control over the project.

It is the same reason that seasoned real estate investors do not invest in pre-contraction condominiums, because we can only bank on appreciation, which is something we have no control over. I am guilty of buying fancy, new, sexy condominiums in the Greater Toronto Area. You are basically giving the builder an interest free loan before you take possession. Who knows if the condominium prices will go up? Who knows if the lending rules will change by the time you take possession? In other words, who knows if you will be able to qualify for the mortgage? Because of the price and condominium fees, a lot of the condos are cash flow negative.

"I can accept failure. Everyone fails at something,
but I cannot accept not trying."
~ **Tony Robbins**

Let me emphasize that this is about control and discipline. Even while writing this book, I fear that I could fail and not finish writing it. However, we could either be defeated and never get up, or let it be the driving force to do more and be better.

"When defeat comes, accept it as a signal that
your plans are not sound. Rebuild those plans,
and set sail once more toward your coveted goals."
~ **Napoleon Hill,** *Think and Grow Rich*

I never lost sleep over the loss. It is still a significant amount of investment for me. However, I know I have tried and made more back through other projects. It is important to constantly remind ourselves why we are investing. We are not deal collectors or property collectors. There is no point of getting into a deal for the sake of doing, and forgetting why we are doing this or what our goals are. This experience did not scare me away from real estate investing. Instead, the experience has taught me to make no impulse purchases going forward, and to consult my mentor and check references in my network. I have since moved on to other projects.

"If you change the way you look at things,
the things you look at change."
~ **Wayne Dyer**

Successful people never treat failure as a negative thing. I saw this online from an unknown source, and I would like to share: *"If you fail, never give up, because F.A.I.L. means FIRST ATTEMPT IN LEARNING. End is not the end. In fact, E.N.D. means EFFORT NEVER DIES. If you get a no as an answer, remember N.O. means NEXT OPPORTUNITY."*

Here is a good exercise you can do on a daily or weekly basis. The point is that failure does not have be a negative notion. Train yourself to focus on the lessons learned. I learned this from Sara Blakely's MasterClass. Write the following statement down and fill in the blanks. This depends on how often you would like to reflect on your lessons learned.

Today or this week, I failed at……………. And I learned that ……………

Remind Yourself to Be Authentic

"Authentic Empowerment:
Power is the alignment of your personality and your soul."
~ Gary Zukav

Unleash the magic that makes you YOU. This is the most important quality I have that helped me to build my network and be where I am today. This power can never be taken away from you. After all, being yourself is the easier thing to do naturally, and this is how people resonate with you. If you are the supporting type, like me, you might have the "disease to please" —saying yes to things you do not feel comfortable doing, but you still do it. I realized that we do not always have to be agreeable. You get to decide that you do not have to say yes to everything. You are not being yourself in that case. If you would want to be of help to others, there is no other way to serve except by being the highest and truest version of yourself.

> *"In order for connection to happen,*
> *we have to allow ourselves to be seen."*
> ~ **Brené Brown**

I have changed the version of this book quite a few times. When I started, I just wanted to put something in the book that would make me look smart, with data or skills I have learned. As I kept going, I realized that I have to be authentic. If it is not the way I normally speak my mind, or if it is not my style, it will not flow very well. It would be a struggle to write this book. More importantly, I do not believe that whoever is reading the book would resonate with me, or I would not be very effective and communicate the ideas that I wanted to convey to you.

You have to work hard toward whatever it is that you are pursuing. However, if you love what you do, it will not feel like work at all. Find your calling. You have to be mindful and present enough to know what works and what feels right. Do what feels right, and follow your instinct. It will just feel like a natural flow to who you are. Of course, you will have to put in a lot of effort, but you will also enjoy the process. It is something you will look forward to doing when you wake up in the morning, especially if you are able to help other people. You can feel it. It is very rewarding. That is one of the reasons I love real estate. Everybody needs a roof above their heads. There are so many different things and strategies you can do with real estate. I am sure you can find something that aligns with your interest and with who you are.

You can use many strategies in real estate investing; you are not restricted to one. Rent to own and private lending are my main investing strategies, and what people in the real estate community know me for. I love doing rent to own, because I do not enjoy renovations or flips. I have done a few to know that it is not in me to manage all the trades, or to know the ins and outs of renovation. There is nothing wrong with that. The end result of doing a flip or fixer-upper is very rewarding. That is why we love to watch HGTV shows. It is just not me or who I am for now.

> *"Be in the flow with what your soul comes to do."*
> **~ Oprah Winfrey**

Many authors have similar ideas to what I have in my book. There is nothing new under the sun. It could be said differently, or in a different story that the readers could relate to. I sometimes overthink and wonder what the point is of me writing if somebody else has already said it, and they are proven to be best-selling authors. I also wonder if there would be something that people know about me that would make it not worth connecting. For example, I am not the one who does the absolute most rent-to-own deals. I know that there are people who have achieved more and have a bigger real estate empire. Well, on the other hand, I can speak to the same idea in my own voice and in my own authentic way. If I can make an impact or have some influence, that is all that matters. The best I can offer, and I believe anyone can offer, is to be uniquely you. That is how people connect.

Brené Brown is the authority on the subject of vulnerability and authenticity. In her most watched Ted Talk, on "the power of vulnerability," she mentioned, "In order for connection to happen, we have to allow ourselves to be seen." I realized that you might be afraid of being successful because it means that you have to put yourself out there. Be authentic and vulnerable in order to connect and be yourself. If you are not happy being yourself, even if you achieve a lot, there is no sense of fulfillment or true accomplishment.

.

Commandment 3: What You Can Do to Get Yourself Ready

Commandment 3

What You Can Do To Get Yourself Ready

&

3

This section is all about mindset. Mindset is everything. You can easily find a bunch of books on each of the topics in Commandment 3.

Gratitude

Always be grateful for any progress you have made in your real estate journey. In this book, I have thanked the people that have made real estate investing an incredible experience for me, or helped me along the way in my life. There are more people I would like to thank, but that would probably take up the whole book.

> *"Be thankful for what you have.*
> *When you focus on the goodness in your life,*
> *you will end up having more."*
> ~ **Oprah Winfrey**

As investors, we always talk about ROI (return on investment). The ROI for gratitude is huge. We are creatures of emotions. When we are grateful, all the good things in our lives, and the positive feelings, amplify. I keep a gratitude journal, and that helps me to consciously look for things to be grateful for. It can also serve as a reminder of how abundant and lucky I am to have the network and support. I can even feel it when I write it down. Being grateful can put you in a calm and happy emotional state. PositivePsychology.com defines gratitude in a way where scientists can measure its effect, and thus argue that gratitude is more than feeling thankful. It is a deeper appreciation for someone or something that produces longer lasting positivity. Like anything else, real estate investing is not always easy. Being grateful to people helping you along the way goes a long way. On the other hand, always be grateful to be in the position to help others as well, because that validates that you are abundant. You are in the position and have the resources to get others to the next level as well, and to pay it forward. That is what you will have when you learn how to create wealth through real estate investing. You will have the superpower to be in the position to help others. When you are grateful, you are abundant.

You can do the bare minimum by just saying "thank you" to your investors, your working partners, or anybody else that helps you get a deal done. It is better than saying nothing. Do a bit more by saying what you are thankful for. Here are a couple of my go-to thank you notes: e.g., thank you for taking the time to answer my questions; thank you for giving me the opportunity to invest with you. What I am truly thankful for is people trusting in me. When investors invest with me, or rent-to-own tenant buyers put in the commitment to come in the program, I usually tell them that they will be in my gratitude journal. People like things written down, such as their name in my gratitude journal, or their name in the foreword of my book, or on a thank-you card. Remember that a person's name, to that person, is the sweetest and most important sound in any language (from the classic book, *How to Win Friends and Influence People,* by Dale Carnegie).

Or why don't you aim to WOW? You can send out a handwritten thank-you card with gift cards, or a bottle of wine for Christmas to your business partners. I send out thank-you cards and Christmas cards to all my tenants every year. Nowadays people are more respectful of different religious backgrounds, or maybe you are too busy buying gifts during the holiday season. Alternatively, you can send out a Happy New Year card. You can also send out personalized gifts. I admit that I love seeing my name on personalized items, such as a mug or a journal.

"Happiness is in front of me
if I am paying attention and practicing gratitude."
~ Brené Brown

I would write or record testimonials for the people that helped me, as a way of showing gratitude, so that more people could benefit from the same training and opportunities that I have received. It is a way of paying it forward, and creates an impact on other people's lives as well. At the same time, I am also grateful for people getting the word out or writing testimonials for me as well.

Getting Inspired and Motivated

Just as with gratitude, getting inspired can put you in a positive mood to take on life. That is why I love success stories. Without being inspired or motivated by people who have done it, or by books on mindsets, it is hard to get started, to take action, or to believe that we have what it takes to succeed.

There were probably around 40 people in the first real estate class I took. As far as I know, only a handful of people (if that) still invest in real estate. It is not surprising, as being an entrepreneur is against the odds anyway. We were all so excited after the class; we exchanged contacts, and I would send out emails to inform people of the upcoming events we could all go to. I was excited to have accountability partners in the class. The momentum was high right after the class. Nevertheless, it quickly died down after we all went back to the real world of working, taking care of kids, or starting to doubt how we would get enough money to kick-start the journey.

I have seen a lot of people give up on real estate investing because they do not see the results right away. However, it is not a get-rich-quick scheme. Most people overestimate what they can do in a year, and underestimate what they can achieve in 10 years. I have heard more than one guru using this line. It is very true. That is why it is so important to keep yourself motivated and to keep the momentum going. Things may not happen right away, but it will happen to you if you are persistent and believe that it will happen. That is why inspiration and motivation are so important to validate your belief. Creating belief and confidence is crucial throughout the process of setting goals, getting motivated, and taking action. The strongest factor for success is self-esteem: believing that you can do it, believing that you will do it, and believing you deserve it.

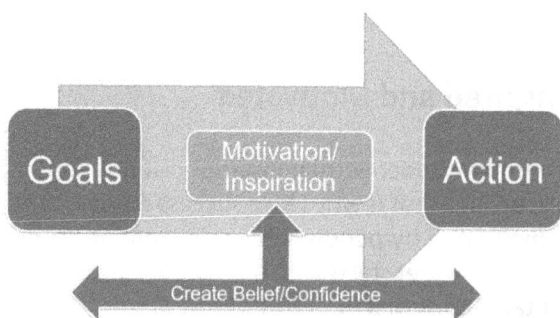

Goals → Motivation/ Inspiration → Action

Create Belief/Confidence

Besides networking, go to meetups to keep yourself motivated, and keep the momentum going. Sometimes you know what you are supposed to do, but you need that little push. You need some inspiration. By now, if you go step by step reading through this book, you should have your goals in front of you, or you should at least know what your goals are and why you are investing in real estate. Your "why" and your goals are strong enough to get you started. And motivation and inspiration is the fuel to prompt you to take action.

"People often say that motivation does not last.
Neither does bathing. That's why we recommend it daily."
~ Zig Ziglar

Physically, people exercise or eat a good breakfast to get the day started. Spiritually, some people meditate. Be in a community of like-minded people. Exchange ideas and experiences to keep each other motivated. Mentally, you can write down in your gratitude journal what you are grateful for. If you want to be really efficient, listen to something inspiring so that you can set the right intention to have an efficient and fulfilling day. Listen to an audiobook. Since I am a slow reader, audiobooks are great alternatives to catch up on reading. For the average millionaire, reading can help them grow and learn. Eighty-five percent of self-made millionaires read two books per month, according to entrepreneur.com. You can find similar data in other sources. Simply, millionaires read!!

Affirmation

Every time you write your affirmation down or say it out loud to yourself, you prime your brain to start believing in your mind. With consistency, you will begin to create the change from within. To tie it in with the last section, "Getting Inspired and Motivated," affirmation is another way to prime yourself.

If you are not sure what you should do, let me make it easy for you.

SAY SOMETHING NICE ABOUT YOURSELF.

I am better today than I was yesterday. Again, I like it simple. This affirmation reminds me to improve in different areas in my life constantly. It also helps me to reflect on how I can develop from what I have experienced, and how I can grow. You can be more specific and be more focused. Ask yourself:

- *Am I a better real estate investor today than I was yesterday?*
- *Do I know more today about real estate than I did a year ago?*

I am smart. I am blessed. I can do anything. There is actually a clip that went viral, where the 3-year-old Ayaan recites, "I am smart. I am blessed. I can do anything," simply on his way to school. He was on the Ellen show and received $20,000 for bringing positivity to millions. If a 3-year-old can do it, you can do it. The simpler the better, because it will be remembered, and it will not take up too much of your precious brainpower.

- *I am an inspiring writer and communicator.*

> **"It is the repetition of affirmations that leads to belief.
> Once that belief becomes a deep conviction,
> things begin to happen."**
> ~ **Muhammad Ali**

MAKE A STATEMENT OF WHAT YOU WANT IN YOUR LIFE.

You can start by saying, **"I am ready for what the Universe is ready to bless me with."** You can also be more specific with what you want.

- *I have a great relationship with money. Money is good, pure, useful, and necessary for my prosperity and growth, and for my satisfaction and well-being. Money brings positive things into my life.*
- *Deals and money will flow naturally and easily to me.*
- *I am committed to the best and truest version of myself.*
- *We found the house that is meant for us.*
- *We are getting the house at a 10% discount.*
- *We are ready to get top dollar for our current home.*

- *We will make it a home that we all want.*
- *The Universe is showing me that we can get what we want.*
- *Thank you, Universe, for making it ours.*
- *I earn $20,000 a month of passive income through real estate investing.*
- *We deserve the new spacious home.*
- *I am living proof that dreams do come true.*

Find a routine that works for you. Find an affirmation that speaks to you and speaks to what you dream about.

Journaling

"Affirmation without discipline is delusion."
~ Jim Rohn

Writing in a journal daily is one of the easiest things you can do to be persistent and have some discipline. You can use the journal to write down what you are grateful for, or as an effective tool to reflect and to record a snapshot of your days, weeks, months, and years.

If you are on the road a lot, keep a small journal with you in your purse. Or if you are a guy without a purse, use your phone to record your ideas. You can think it, say it, or write it down. I find that writing it down is the most effective way to see your thoughts come to life, and to solidify your ideas. Richard Branson, the founder of Virgin, has said that he would not have been able to build Virgin without the help of a simple notebook. Write everything down. This is a million-dollar lesson that I did not learn in business school.

In order to help others, I know I have be to be in a good state and feel peace in my heart. I know I have to be at my best to serve, and for my own sake as well. Otherwise, it would not be fair to those who invest their time with me in reading the book or getting coaching from me. With all the challenges and things going on in life, it is not always an easy task. What I found is that journaling really helps to free my mind of time management and goal setting. I highly recommend "The Five Minute Journal" if you want a system and a simple way to be effective and be happier. Sometimes it does not even take five minutes to write the journal. The only thing not included in "The Five Minute Journal" is a place to write down your goals daily. I have a short list of goals that I write down every day. I admit that I am not perfect, and I am not always at my 100% best, but journaling definitely helps.

As a matter of fact, you do not even need to buy a specific journal. Freestyle! Any pretty notebook will do. I would include the following sections in it to make the best use of journaling. Note that I do not include my daily to-do list in my journal. It is a personal choice, and it is up to you. I write my to-do list on a separate piece of scrap paper and recycle it once completed. A to-do list is a good tool to help you prioritize and focus on completing the tasks for the day. The reason I do not put it in my journal is that I consider a to-do list to be a list of tasks. I go to my journal to reflect and for self-learning. I do not want to have a list of tasks cluttering the pages when I go back to it. Remembering to deposit a rent check, or to call the credit card company to clarify a payment, really does not serve me in a constructive way once done.

Date: _____

I am grateful for:

(Most gratitude journals suggest listing 3 things you are grateful for. I would suggest listing 5 things you are grateful for. Raise the bar a bit higher.)

1. _____

2. _____

3. _____

4. _____

5. _____

Affirmation – Today I am:

_____

Find a good quote or quotes for inspiration for today:

_____

Goals:

_____

Notes:

_____

_____

Commandment 4

Lease Options (Rent-to-Own)

&

f you have diligently read this book page by page, you might be thinking... let's get to it already. The purpose of all the prep work so far is to figure out what you really want out of real estate investing, and what it could really do for you to achieve your goals and dreams. Having the right mindset goes a long way. Constantly remind yourself to possess the quality of being grateful, mindful, and authentic.

Why is mindset so important in real estate investing? The concept is simple. However, it is not easy. If it was easy, everybody would do it. Financial education is not taught in school. When we talk about investing or money, it sometimes makes people feel uncomfortable. That is why I believe it is imperative for you to go through the section of this book on getting out of your comfort zone and getting yourself mentally ready. Be persistent, get over self-doubt, and take action.

Consider the following when searching for a good real estate deal. Please underline, highlight, or triple-star these important investment objectives.

- **Cash flow is king:** As an investor, treat your real estate investing as a business. You want to continue to grow your portfolio. It is not sustainable when there is negative cash flow.

- **ROI (return on investment):** Return on investment is an important concept when looking at creating wealth. The rule of 72 is a good tool to use. It gives you an idea of the timeline required to double your investment. For example, if you want to double your investment, at 6% interest rate, it will take you 12 years. (72/6). Imagine if you were getting 12% interest, which is achievable through real estate investing; you would only need 6 years to double your investment.

- **Make money in the buy**: There are a lot of opportunities around. Do not over pay, and always look for money in the buy, to ensure that you are winning at the starting line.

Now let's look at steps to take to get you there. We have gone through finding your goals, in the earlier section of this book. Let's get into different strategies and how to find the strategy that fits your goals. After you find your goal, to get started, the next step is to find a strategy that will help you reach your goals. We call it "Goal, SMP" (strategy, market, and then property) at Trust Your Talent, where I am currently coaching. With the strategy in mind, find a market that makes sense to use the strategy in. Finally, look for a property in that market. Your strategy depends on what you want to achieve.

Basically, there are three buckets of income.

- **Earned income:** working income, such as job and wholesale, where you are actively looking for deals.

- **Passive income:** Collecting rent, dividends, or interest, for example.

- **Portfolio income:** Equity in a property.

You can have income in all three buckets. When you have enough income generated from all three buckets, that could replace your income, and you could quit your job—you have reached *"financial independence."* On the other hand, when you have enough *passive income* to cover all your expenses, you have reached *"financial freedom."*

Whether your goal is to reach *financial freedom* so that you do not have to worry about retirement, or *financial independence* so that you can fire your boss—or simply have the option to—and not have to worry about job security, lease options is a strategy that can help you reach these goals. You will see how it works when we go through the numbers.

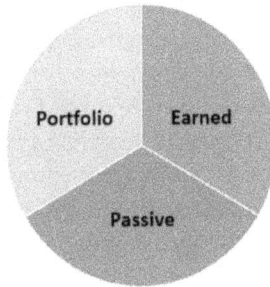

An untrained investor often looks for a property first, and then tries to solve the problem of negative cash flow, tenant management issues, etc. Again, it should be the other way around: goals, SMP (strategy, market, and then property). If your goal is to have great cash flow, a good return, and to capture the benefits of appreciation, then a lease option, which is also known as rent-to-own, is a good strategy for you.

I might be partial since this is the strategy I focused on to help me reach my goals. Lease options have given me the opportunity to help future homeowners, and have eliminated a lot of tenant management headaches. As an investor, you are able to gain control and get an amazing return and cash flow with this strategy.

When I started working on getting qualified tenant buyers, I talked to roughly 100 potential leads per qualified tenant buyer. That is a 1% rate. It does not seem very efficient, does it? By hearing me go through so many calls, I am pretty sure that my husband, Doug, could get on a call to screen tenant buyers as well. Nevertheless, that was a great learning opportunity. My calls to tenant buyer leads would last 45 minutes or longer—listening to them complain about life not being fair—when it would really only take 15 minutes to get all the information I would need.

Now I mainly get my deals from wholesalers or referrals from my network. You may not have to pay for wholesale fees or referrals if you look for tenant buyers on your own. Hey, but look at the big picture. Think about how much time you can save. Focus on what you are good at. There are other people who have more time or are better at marketing to find potential tenant buyers than I am. Even if you have to pay a referral fee/finder's fee (whatever you want to call it), or share equity, remember that "50% of something is better than 100% of nothing." This is what my mentor always says.

On the other hand, countless times, I have also explained lease options to my investors, students, or people who are just interested. With my experience in talking to people about lease options, my goal for you is to leverage my knowledge and experience. In this section, we will go through the strategy in a comprehensive way that covers what you need to know if you are interested in getting started in lease options. I mostly use the term "lease options" instead of "rent-to-own," so that you will think like an investor, and not be confused with rent-to-own office furniture, for example. However, it is considered a more advanced strategy. Every lease option deal is different. Every tenant buyer's situation is unique. This is also my mentor's baby strategy that helped him reach his goal of financial freedom. I have gone through advanced training and followed my mentor's guidance. If this is what you are truly interested in, it is worth it to invest in your education, apply the knowledge, and take action to make it your baby strategy too.

What Is a Lease Option?

A lease option is a lease agreement with an option to purchase at the end of a term of typically 2–4 years. Note that it is an option. Tenants have the right to buy, but it is up to the tenants to decide whether or not to exercise the option. Optionees, or tenant buyers, are tenants first and foremost in the process. They turn into buyers once they are qualified and choose to buy. There are different types of lease option strategies, including *tenant first* and *property first* lease option strategies. In this section, I will focus on *tenant first* lease options. In a lease option program, we call the tenants *tenant buyers* because the goal is to guide them on the journey from being renters to being homeowners. With the help of our power team, including mortgage brokers, my investors, my business partners, realtors, credit specialists, and so on, we help tenant buyers qualify for a mortgage and save up enough down payment to buy the property of their choice.

You may like the idea of *property first* lease options, since it means "no money down deals," and this is how we, as investors, can grow quickly without the limitation of looking for funds or mortgages. *Property first* means that the owner of the property may be willing to offer the property up for a lease option deal. We then find a tenant buyer that is interested in the property, in the exact market, who would like to make that exact property their home.

Going back to SMP (strategy, market, and property), it is not impossible; but *property first*, in my opinion, is not easy to do. I am open to the idea, but this is not my focus. There will be vacancy when you are waiting for the right tenant buyers to fit in the property. There is vacancy and holding cost while looking for a good tenant buyer for the property. Location is fixed. One of the main reasons that a lease option is such an attractive strategy to the tenant buyer, is that they get to choose the property that fits their requirements. It is like an arranged marriage. A *property first* lease option strategy limits the tenants to the house we are trying to match them with.

Tenant Buyer First	Property First
• Zero Vacancy and no holding cost • Tenants choose the market and property • Purchase price fits tenant's budget	• Vacancy • Location and property fixed • Harder to match property to tenant buyers • Sandwich lease option: low to no money down

I prefer the *tenant buyer first* strategy, where we qualify the tenant buyers first. We give them a budget and let them know when they qualify for a mortgage, and then they have the option to buy the property of their choice. The first exciting part for the tenant buyers is for them to shop for a home of their choice. It is easier to match their requirements to a home than the other way around.

I am usually pretty flexible with the location as long as the property makes sense. I would make it clear to the tenant buyers that we do not want to buy a property that is falling apart, is not insurable, or if the bank would not provide a mortgage on it. We will not buy houses with roof or foundation issues. This is not a fix and flip strategy. I would try to avoid condominiums with expensive maintenance fees as well, because when tenant buyers qualify for a mortgage, a condo fee of roughly $450 will take away about $100,000 of their mortgage room. As for us as investors, there is no vacancy and there is no holding cost. We have tenants for the investment property as soon as we close on the property.

Lease and Option Contracts

A lease option consists of two contracts. The lease agreement is not that different from a regular lease. In Ontario, we are using the Standard Ontario Lease. Usually, we do not increase the rent annually in a lease option deal. Tenant buyers pay at least market rent to cover PITI, which is principal, interest (i.e., mortgage), property tax, and insurance. Tenant buyers pay for all utilities and repairs. Nonetheless, make sure tenant buyers do not overspend on repairs and renovation. Our goal is to make sure they have enough to support the monthly payment and not further bruise their credit.

In addition, there is the option contract that states the tenant buyer's right of first refusal to purchase the property at a specific price and on a specific date. If it is a 3-year rent-to-own program, the purchase date would be the end of the 3-year lease. The option contract will also include the rights and obligations of the optionees/tenant buyers and optionors/property owners. Disclaimer: I am not a lawyer, so I am explaining this section in plain English so that you, as an investor and not a lawyer, can easily understand as well.

Tenant buyers have to come in with an initial option consideration. In order for a contract to be valid, there has to be money exchanging hands. Tenant buyers come in with initial option consideration to start the program. On top of that, tenant buyers also contribute to monthly option consideration. Both initial and monthly option consideration will be converted to down payment when the tenant buyers are qualified for a mortgage and are ready to buy.

Lease	Option
• A lease for the duration of the program	• Tenant buyers come in with initial option consideration

• Tenant buyers pay market rents
  • Pay for all repairs
  • Pay for all utilities
	• Additional monthly payments that will be converted to down payment

	• Gives tenant buyers the option to purchase the property

Nobody has a crystal ball to predict which direction the market will go. As an investor, you might be wondering what to do if the property value goes down. What happens when the property value goes up significantly? We are in the real estate investing game for the long haul. Do everything ethically. Even when the property value goes up significantly, tenant buyers can still buy the property at the agreed price stated in the option contract.

I am currently investing in Southern Ontario, in cities such as Toronto, Barrie, Kingston, Peterborough, London, Oshawa, Orangeville, and so on. Luckily, for all the lease options, property values have gone up significantly. This means that there is already equity in the deals for the tenant buyers by the time they are ready to purchase. Tenant buyers can buy the house they live in, and with equity in the house, we have already helped them to generate wealth through real estate. Tenant buyers will be more motivated to work toward home-ownership in a hot market.

On the other hand, what happens when the price goes down? There are several ways you can structure your lease option deals to be more protected during the down turn.

• Tenant buyers can continue to rent. All my lease option deals still cash flow with just the lease income.

- Tenant buyers can walk away from the deal, but they will not be able to get full refund of the option deposit. We will use the option deposit to sell the property, and to pay the realtor's commission and other costs associated with closing. This is the same idea as banks or alternative lenders that require a down payment when you purchase a property. If you stop paying your mortgage or walk away from the property, you will not get a refund of your down payment if your lenders end up selling your house. The mortgage default rate is around 1% or 2% in Canada. People normally do not just give up what they have already put their hard-earned money into.

- Tenant buyers give up the right to purchase when they miss any lease or option payments. It is important for tenant buyers to understand that when signing the contracts.

Tenant Buyer Profile

You might be wondering why we would choose to help the tenant buyers when the banks would not approve their mortgages. Not everybody who wants to be a homeowner or wants to get out of a rental, is suitable for lease option. There are three criteria to qualify for a mortgage.

1. Good credit
2. Stable income
3. Enough down payment

We may be able to fix and monitor tenant buyers' bruised credits. They might be newcomers, self-employed, or have bruised their credit due to a divorce. They just need time to build their credit scores up. We can help them save up the option deposit, which will be converted to a down payment when tenant buyers are ready to buy. The only thing we do not help tenant buyers with is finding a job with stable income, even though sometimes I do feel the urge to help them find a better job as well.

Helping One Family at a Time to Become Homeowners

What I love about lease options is that it is a people's business. Every tenant buyer has a different story. I have many stories to share when it comes to tenant buyers. I was filled with gratitude when I took these pictures. Although I have talked about all the benefits of a lease option strategy, the spirit of the strategy is to help tenant buyers own the house at the end of the program. There is a lot of negative news about lease options. Their friends and families could be the naysayers, telling them not to trust us, and showing them the negative news online. Investors can take their money and sell the property under them, or sell the property on the market if it appreciates more than the option purchase price. That is also why we want to do this right—so we can be in it for the long haul and continue to help people, and make a good profit at the same time, with our knowledge in real estate investing. Tenant buyers place tremendous trust in us when they hand over the initial option deposit and commit to the program.

To give you an idea who our tenant buyers are, what their families are like, and what situations they are in, here are some of their stories. I am not using their real names, for privacy reasons.

- Neil and Ellen are new immigrants with two young kids. When they started the program, they had no credit and just needed some time to build their credit as newcomers. Neil is a bus driver working night shifts, and Ellen works in a daycare. They are a hard-working couple who desperately want to buy a home, but they do not have the credit yet, or enough money saved for the down payment they would need. They decided to do a lease option on a nice home in Kingston, Ontario.

- Christy has a big family. She was not educated on how to maintain a good credit score while supporting her big family. She has three kids, and her parents live with her. Christy's father co-signed on the lease and option contracts since they are all living together. Her husband, as a newcomer, needs some time to build his credit as well. We purchased a starter home, with three bedrooms and a den, for the family of seven, in Barrie, Ontario.

They are on track to improve their credit and complete the program in three years. By the end of the program, we will be able to sell the property, with no sales commission, to the family.

- Nina came from the Philippines. She was separated from her family for many years, working abroad in Hong Kong, Taiwan, and Canada. She bruised her credit going through the immigration process and flying her family over to Canada. She was able to find jobs for her husband and two adult kids, at the facility she works at. Her younger kid started college in Canada and is working part time at a Tim Hortons. They are a hard-working family. Within a week of landing in Canada, the family started working.

With their hard-working ethics and the number of adults in the family working, they will be able to qualify for the mortgage once they build their credit. The investors and tenant buyers were all very patient throughout the process to get this deal done. We are all grateful for working together as a great team and creating a win-win deal for everybody involved. After putting in several offers on different properties, we finally purchased a home for the family, in Orangeville, Ontario.

- Johnny was divorced and moved into the lease option property with his girlfriend to have a fresh start. He is handy and wants to have a fresh start. He has a little girl, so we purchased an older and smaller house for him to move into with his girlfriend, with a bedroom for his little girl as well. We were able to find him a property just outside of Kingston, Ontario, which was affordable and he could work on improving.

Tenant buyers can usually renovate or decorate the property. The property is still under the investor's name, so I would ask the tenants to inform us when they want to make major changes to the house. In general, we are open to tenants improving the property to make it feel like home. I only ask the tenants to not overspend to the point that it will affect their credit or ability to save up. When the places feel like home, tenant buyers would have a bigger drive to succeed and work harder toward the goal of homeownership. Tenants choose their home in the market they want to be in. In addition, we are pet-friendly. This is another advantage for the tenant buyers.

It seems like a lot to save up for the tenant buyers, considering they will have to come up with the option consideration and monthly rent as well. However, saving is never easy. This is what it takes to come up with a down payment for a family. If you are buying a property in a city like Toronto or Vancouver, imagine how much and how long it would take an average homeowner to save up. Affordability is an issue, and major banks release reports on the subject quarterly. That is beyond the scope of this section. The point I am trying to make here is that tenant buyers usually have stable jobs and good household income to be able to afford being in the program.

Let's Run the Numbers

Now let's get to the numbers. This is a very exciting part of lease options. A lease option is such a creative financing strategy. Not only do we help tenant buyers, we are also making good profit and cash flow by doing so. You can generate a fantastic cash flow, a good return, and money in the buy, in a lease option deal.

How Do We Determine the Option Consideration?

Being a seasoned real estate investor is about control. The option purchase price is defined. Although the property value likely will go up more than the option purchase price, we have more control over the return on investment and tenant buyers' abilities to exercise the option to purchase.

The goal is to help the tenant buyers save up to at least 10% of the purchase price by the end of the program. This aligns with what we discussed in the earlier section on goal setting. By having something to aim for, tenant buyers will have a greater chance of success. Assuming that the buy-back price of the property is $500,000, and the tenant buyers come in the program with $26,000 of initial option consideration, and if it is a 2-year rent-to-own program, that means tenant buyers will save up to a total of $50,000, which is 10% of $500,000. Since the tenant buyers put in an initial option consideration of $26,000, they will save up another $24,000 during the 2-year period. Therefore, their monthly option consideration will be $2,000. ($24,000/12 months).

I am using very simple numbers here to give you an idea on how to come up with the monthly option consideration. Let's look at an actual example of a lease option deal that I have completed. I aim to simplify the numbers to demonstrate how it works. As mentioned earlier, we are looking for these elements in a real estate investment deal.

- **Cash flow is king.**
- **ROI (return on investment).**
- **Make money in the buy.**

Therefore, we can now get into how lease options accomplished these objectives.

Example: Rent to Own in Orangeville ON

- Purchase price: $470,000 (3 year term)
- Option to purchase price: $544,100 (Appreciating at 5% per year)
- Initial Option: $15,000
- Total $3,750 per month (Rent of $2,400 and Monthly Option of $1,150)
- Cash flow $1,650 per month

I have rounded off the numbers in this example. We will arrive at the ROI as we go through the calculation of this deal. This is a typical starter home, with 3 bedrooms and 2 baths, in Southern Ontario. The tenant buyer came with an initial option consideration of $15,000, so the closing cost is reduced. That is where *we make money in the buy*.

Cash Flow:

- Monthly Option + Rent: $1,150+$2,400 = $3,550
  - Monthly option: (Option: 10% of option price – Initial Option)/36 months
- Expenses: Mortgage, Property Tax, Insurance = $1,900
- Monthly Cash Flow: $1,650   (Cash flow over 3-yr term: $59,400)

Cash flow is king. As shown in the calculation, we are collecting $3,550 per month. After all expenses are paid, there is a **cash flow** of $1,650.

Profit From Sale:

Sale Price: $544,100

Less: Mortgage balance: $350,000

      Legal Cost: $1,600

      Initial Investment: DP + Land Transfer + Lawyer fee – IOC: $86,500

      Total Option Consideration: $56,400

• (No agent commission)

                Total Profit from Sale: $49,600

There is no realtor involved at the end of the program when tenant buyers decide to exercise their option to purchase. We appreciate the property at 5% per year in this case. After the mortgage balance and all other expenses are paid, the profit from the sale is close to fifty thousand dollars.

Deal Summary:

• **Total Profit:** Cash Flow + Profit from Sale

= $59,400 +$49,600= $109,000

• **Annual ROI:** Total Profit/Initial Investment/3 years

            = $109,000/$86,500/3

            = 42% simple int/ yr. (21% per JV)

In this case, the total **return on investment (ROI)** of the deal is 42%. Because it is a 50/50 split joint venture deal, my investor and I are able to enjoy a return of 21% after all initial investment and expenses are paid.

Every deal is different, and every tenant buyer's situation is unique. Typically, I would aim for a 15% ROI, and more for my investors. When you look at these numbers, wouldn't you want to be involved in more deals like this?

Let's recap.

- **Cash flow is king**. In this case, there is a total cash flow of $1,650 per month, and that is $825 per JV partner.
- **ROI (return on investment)**. The total return on this deal is 42%, so 21% per JV partner.
- **Make money in the buy**. The initial option consideration is $15,000.

Compound Effect of Lease Options

When my mentor first showed me what focusing on just one strategy, lease options, can do, it totally blew my mind. F.O.C.U.S.: follow one course until success. Let's use the same example to explain what this strategy can do for you, toward building wealth and financial freedom or financial independence for you to achieve your dreams.

Assume that we are using the same deal we went through in the previous section, as a 3 to 5 year plan. You are still working and can only devote part-time effort to real estate investing. In this deal, the property is purchased at $470,000. It is a 3-year lease option deal. The tenant buyer started the program with $15,000 of initial option consideration.

In year one, you did one deal per quarter or per season. As demonstrated here, you will get $1,650 of cash flow per month, and collect $15,000 as each tenant buyer starts the program. You are able to enjoy the monthly cash flow from January for the first deal, April for the second deal, and so on and so forth. Because my lease option deals are usually structured as a 50/50 joint venture, we each get half of the income, which is $51,450 for each party.

If you rinse and repeat the same process, using the same strategy in year two, you will be able to enjoy the cash flow of the first four deals for the full year, adding the cash flow and collecting more initial option consideration in the second year. The assumption is the same: a part-time effort and you find a deal each quarter.

Year 1		
Deal 1 (Completed in January)		
Intial Option Consideration	....	$ 15,000
Cash Flow ($1,650 x 11M)	....	$ 18,150
Deal 2 (Completed in April)		
Intial Option Consideration	....	$ 15,000
Cash Flow ($1,650 x 8M)	....	$ 13,200
Deal 3 (Completed in July)		
Intial Option Consideration	....	$ 15,000
Cash Flow ($1,650 x 5M)	....	$ 8,250
Deal 4 (Completed in October)		
Intial Option Consideration	....	$ 15,000
Cash Flow ($1,650 x 2M)	....	$ 3,300
Total income in Year 1		
Money in the buy (IOC)		**$ 60,000**
Cash Flow:		**$ 42,900**
Total income in Year 1		**$102,900**
50/50 JV		**$ 51,450**
IOC: Initial Option Consideration		

Year 2		
Cash Flow from the 4 deals in Year 1		
($1,650 x 12M x 4 deals)	....	$ 79,200
Deal 5 (Completed in January)		
Intial Option Consideration	....	$ 15,000
Cash Flow ($1,650 x 11M)	....	$ 18,150
Deal 6 (Completed in April)		
Intial Option Consideration	....	$ 15,000
Cash Flow ($1,650 x 8M)	....	$ 13,200
Deal 7 (Completed in July)		
Intial Option Consideration	....	$ 15,000
Cash Flow ($1,650 x 5M)	....	$ 8,250
Deal 8 (Completed in October)		
Intial Option Consideration	....	$ 15,000
Cash Flow ($1,650 x 2M)	....	$ 3,300
Total income in Year 2		
Money in the buy (IOC)		**$ 60,000**
Cash Flow:		**$122,100**
Total income in Year 2		**$182,100**
50/50 JV		**$ 91,050**

Repeat the same course of action on a part-time basis in the third year. Assuming that you are getting another four deals and enjoying a full year of cash flow from the first eight deals, your third year income will grow by more than 30%. If you are working full time, how often do you get a 30% raise annually?

In the fourth year is when you receive the profits from selling the properties, when the tenant buyers exercise their options to purchase. Besides the cash flow and initial option consideration, you are also profiting from the sales of the properties. Your income almost doubled from year 3 to year 4.

Year 3

Cash Flow from the 8 deals in Year 1 & 2		
($1,650 x 12M x 8 deals)	....	$ 158,400
Deal 9 (Completed in January)		
Intial Option Consideration	....	$ 15,000
Cash Flow ($1,650 x 11M)	....	$ 18,150
Deal 10 (Completed in April)		
Intial Option Consideration	....	$ 15,000
Cash Flow ($1,650 x 8M)	....	$ 13,200
Deal 11 (Completed in July)		
Intial Option Consideration	....	$ 15,000
Cash Flow ($1,650 x 5M)	....	$ 8,250
Deal 12 (Completed in October)		
Intial Option Consideration	....	$ 15,000
Cash Flow ($1,650 x 2M)	....	$ 3,300
Total income in Year 3		
Money in the buy (IOC)		**$ 60,000**
Cash Flow:		**$ 201,300**
Total income in Year 2		**$ 261,300**
50/50 JV		$ 130,650

Year 4

Deal 1 Profit from closing		$ 49,600
Deal 2 Profit from closing		$ 49,600
Deal 2 Cash flow ($1,650 x 3M)		$ 4,950
Deal 3 Profit from closing		$ 49,600
Deal 3 Cash flow ($1,650 x 6M)		$ 9,900
Deal 4 profit from closing		$ 49,600
Deal 4 Cash flow ($1,650 x 9M)		$ 14,850
Cash Flow from deals 5-12		
($1,650 x 12M x 8 deals)	....	$ 158,400
Deal 9 (Completed in January)		
Intial Option Consideration	....	$ 15,000
Cash Flow ($1,650 x 11M)	....	$ 18,150
Deal 10 (Completed in April)		
Intial Option Consideration	....	$ 15,000
Cash Flow ($1,650 x 8M)	....	$ 13,200
Deal 11 (Completed in July)		
Intial Option Consideration	....	$ 15,000
Cash Flow ($1,650 x 5M)	....	$ 8,250
Deal 12 (Completed in October)		
Intial Option Consideration	....	$ 15,000
Cash Flow ($1,650 x 2M)	....	$ 3,300
Total income in Year 4		
Money in the buy (IOC)		$ 60,000
Cash Flow:		$ 231,000
Total income in Year 4		**$ 489,400**
50/50 JV		$ 244,700

We have gone through an advanced real estate investment strategy in just one chapter. I could write a whole book on this subject, so the purpose here is to provide a guide on how it works, and the benefits of using the strategy. I have taken an advanced course and a refresher on lease options. I started by working with wholesalers and other experienced lease option investors.

More importantly, I had a mentor guiding me along the way. I highly recommend that you do the same if you plan to use the strategy. The best way of compressing your time to be financially free in a "royal way," is to have a mentor accelerate your path to success, with his or her experience and expertise. Even the best of the best in the world continue to hire coaches and mentors. You do not need to reinvent the wheel. Do it right and do it ethically.

Exercise:
Are Lease Options the right investment strategy for you?

Review the three buckets of income, and list what you have right now and what you would like to have to achieve your goals.

Financial Goals:
For me to reach my financial goals, I need to generate $_____ per month.

Buckets of income you currently have and/or require to achieve your financial goals:

Active/earned income: _____

Passive income: _____

Portfolio income: _____

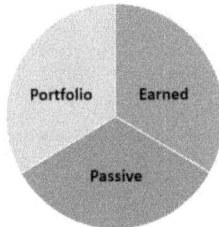

Considering your goals and the pros and cons, are lease options a good strategy for you? Why or why not?

_____

_____

Commandment 5

Wholesale

A t my very first real estate investing seminar, I remember that the speaker said, a few times, "There is no reason why any of you cannot start wholesaling today." I thought: *why would I want to wholesale? Why do I need to learn about wholesaling? I would like to create more passive income instead of active income through real estate.* However, I later learned that wholesaling is not limited to finding ugly houses to fix and flip. I have wholesaled my deals. In addition, I am working with wholesalers for my lease option deals, and I do private lending deals with flippers/wholesalers as well. The reason I am devoting this chapter to wholesaling is that this is a strategy that every real estate investor will use throughout their real estate investing career. Because there is no reason why any newbies cannot start wholesaling today, it is also where a lot of new investors start getting into real estate.

The concept is simple, and it does not just apply to real estate investing. Buy something at a lower price than what you can sell it for. You hunt for good deals, negotiate a deep discount, put together a contract, and finally sell it or assign it to someone else. If you are considering wholesaling, your network is particularly important to you. Your network determines your net worth, whether you need a bird dog (somebody looking for deals for you), OPM (other people's money) to finance the renovation of the houses you found, or people on your buyer's list to assign your wholesale deals to.

To assign a contract means that you are passing the purchase agreement or contract on to somebody else. Wholesalers usually get a deal under contract, meaning having control over the deal first. Then they assign the contract to the buyer, with a fee.

Advantages of Wholesaling

You can consider focusing on wholesaling if these benefits are what you are looking for.

- No money down
- Close fast, quick profit
- No credit history required
- Control without ownership
- Do not need a license
- Flexible hours
- A tool to have in your toolbox, as you will use this strategy in your entire investing career

Getting your name on the deed to a property is not your goal. Your goal is to find deals that make you money. Assign the deal to your buyer for a fee. It could be called an assignment fee, wholesale fee, or finder's fee.

The bigger the problem, usually the more profit you can make from the deal. Here are some situations where you could help the sellers and solve their problems for them.

- Going through a divorce.
- Having financial problems, and in need of getting cash and out of the property quickly.
- Tired landlords with problem tenants.
- Properties with issues that the owners do not want to take care of.
- Financing rules changed. Buyers were not approved for a mortgage.

All real estate investors will touch upon wholesaling, whether they are wholesaling their deals when they have too many opportunities on hand to take them all on, or they are buying deals from other people when they are actively looking for a project to work on. Keep in mind that a good wholesale deal:

1. **ALWAYS makes money in the buy.**
2. **Leaves something on the table for the next person.**
3. **Makes it a WIN-WIN: provides solutions to problems. The bigger the problem, the greater the profit.**

Typical Wholesale Deals

When you think of "wholesale," do you picture somebody who is a flipper and knows how to market for good deals? That makes sense. Because a wholesaler finds an underpriced property or a property with potential, he or she can keep it, flip it, or sell it as is. The buyers can buy it at a discount **(make money in the buy)**, perhaps renovate it, and increase the value of the property. Buyers can flip the house and make a profit as well. The uglier the house, the higher the potential. In other words, the bigger the problem, the higher the profit.

A wholesaler might be solving the problem of a tired property owner, for example. Flippers and wholesalers are usually familiar with big renovation projects, and they know how much and how long a typical flip will take. When flippers have too many projects on the go, or it is more profitable to just wholesale the contract to somebody else, then they could choose to do so. You do not need a realtor's license to be a wholesaler. It is listed as an advantage of doing wholesale and assignment. However, some wholesalers do have realtor's licenses. It makes sense when you have the volume and could save on sales commissions.

You can wholesale a property in up, down, or sideways markets. You can wholesale properties anywhere, in declining or up and coming areas, to bring up values. Money will follow good deals. Here are some guidelines on what a good deal could look like:

- Usually buy 40%–70% below market value (30–60 cents to the dollar)
- Abandoned, vacant, problem properties
- May not be able to get traditional financing
- Great opportunities for investors

Remember that you are still following the same principles of a wholesale deal. There is money in the buy. You are leaving some meat on the bone for the next person. Additionally, you are a problem solver using different real estate investing strategies.

Determining fair market value (FMV), or after repair value (AFV), is an extremely important part of the wholesale process. You need to know your market and the potential FMV or AFV before you can assess if you are within the 40%–70% below market value guideline. Also, you need to know the numbers before you can wholesale your option to the property, to your buyers.

The realtors on your power team are able to pull the information for you. Depending on the market, you are looking for recent data on comparable properties sold within the last 3–6 months. Comparables, for example, are properties of the same type (e.g., duplexes, single-family homes, etc.), in the same area, with similar square footage.

On the next page is an example of a typical flip, which I was involved in with a flipper. I have altered and simplified the numbers of the actual deal, for learning purposes.

The property was acquired at $230,000. If you look at the price the property was sold at, it is not within the "30 to 60 cents to the dollar" guideline. Perhaps we overestimated the ARV. In this case, would you still do the deal? It is your decision as an investor. I would! Despite the fact that it was not purchased at a huge discount, it was not a big

Fleming, London ON			
Sales Price	$	365,000	
Purchase Price	$	230,000	63.0%
Renos	$	35,000	72.6%
Carrying Cost	$	19,875	
Legal Fees	$	2,000	
Commission	$	19,000	
Total Profit	**$**	**59,125**	

- 63 cents to the dollar
- With Reno: 72.6 cents to the dollar

renovation project, and it could be completed in a relatively short timeframe. The point I am trying to make here is that it is a guideline. There are other factors to consider. As you can see, there is still good profit to be made here.

To mitigate risk and have control as a seasoned real estate investor, **always make sure you have two or more exit strategies**. This property was actually designed to be a student rental. There are six bedrooms in total. We could either sell it or keep it as a student rental. There would be a good cash flow. We ended up selling the property, and we made a quick profit by flipping it—but remember: **Always make sure you have two or more exit strategies.**

Examples of Different Types of Wholesale Deals

You can wholesale single-family homes, apartments, commercial buildings, or raw land. You can also wholesale lease option deals.

The lease option is the strategy I focus on. Since we have gone through lease options previously, you can see how we can combine different strategies. This is the property in Midland, Ontario. I did not find a joint venture partner and keep the first lease option deal I had. Instead, I wholesaled the deal to a fellow investor. I learned a lot during the process. I put up an ad on Kijiji and qualified the tenant buyer using an investor friendly mortgage broker, as I was trained to do in class. Being my first lease option deal, shortly after I took my lease option class, I was excited to see what I learned come to life. I was excited that I got to practice what I had rehearsed at my mentorship, but I was still quite nervous as a newbie. Everything happened so fast, and I was blessed that I had found an investor who was trained the same way and spoke the same language in real estate investing.

Keep in mind that a good wholesale deal:

1. **ALWAYS makes money in the buy.**
2. **Leaves something on the table for the next person.**
3. **Makes it a WIN-WIN: provides solutions to problems. The bigger the problem, the greater the profit.**

Since the tenant buyer contributed the initial option consideration, and helped with the closing cost, there is money in the buy. In this case, my wholesale fee is 60% of the initial option consideration, so I have left something on the table for my investor. I received my wholesale fee, and my investor had a lease option deal with good returns. On top of that, the investor continues to collect monthly rent and monthly option consideration. Tenant buyers picked a property of their choice and were able to work on fixing their credit for the time being. The most important thing is that I know the tenants are in good hands. It is a multiple WIN for everybody involved.

This example shows that the wholesale strategy is not limited to be used on ugly and smelly houses with roof and foundation problems. The wholesale strategy could be used with other strategies as well. Being a seasoned real estate investor is about control and solving problems. Put it under contract. In other words, control the project or the property when you have it under contract.

Remember your "goal, SMP (strategy, market, and property)," as we emphasized in the previous chapter. As a wholesaler, it is also critical for you to know what your buyers are looking for and what their "goals, SMPs" are.

Tips on Marketing

By now, you know that a successful wholesaler has the ability to consistently find great deals and:

1. **ALWAYS make money in the buy.**
2. **Leave something on the table for the next person.**
3. **Make it a WIN-WIN: provide solutions to problems. The bigger the problem, the greater the profit.**

The fact is that not all deals are good deals. I have seen wholesalers advertise deals that do not meet all these criteria. Your reputation is important for the longevity of your real estate investing journey. Make sure you do your due diligence to find great deals. It is possible to find them. Successful wholesalers I have met are either marketing geniuses or amazing networkers.

Direct Mail: You can send mail to a targeted list of sellers, assuming that a small percentage of your targeted audience will respond and you will find a motivated seller. It could be very costly, so make sure your marketing campaign stands out and catches the audience's attention.

Bird dogs: It is a term used for hunting. Let people know that you are wholesaling and looking for deals. Your bird dogs can be your realtors, your neighbors, or even the pizza delivery boy, as long as they know what is going on in the neighborhood. They can spot a deal for you, for a finder's fee. Empower your network and leverage other people's time. You can also co-wholesale a deal with another wholesaler if you have investors or buyers lined up.

Driving or Walking Around: Go around the neighborhood that you are interested in. You might be able to spot a boarded-up house, or a property with long grass or broken windows. The advantage is that it costs very little to drive around or go for a walk in the neighborhood.

Find a way to get in touch with the owner. Maybe talk to the tenants or the neighbors to get in touch with the owners and get the property under contract.

FSBO (For Sale by Owner): Some homeowners simply do not want to clean up the house or list their properties with an agent. Homeowners often price their properties too high, but if you can buy with cash, help them close quickly, and provide a hassle-free solution, you will find willing sellers.

Advertise on Kijiji or Craigslist: It is easy, and it is cost efficient. These sites are free unless you are investing in making your ad stand out or being on top of the search list. Kijiji has also started to limit the number of ads allowed by one user. Nevertheless, it is worth a few minutes to post an ad. Get your business name and phone number out there.

Set up a Website: Wholesalers are problem solvers. Again, *the bigger the problem, the greater the profit.* When motivated sellers have problems, they are likely to get on Google and look for solutions. Good wholesalers are often very good marketers. It takes great effort to learn the algorithms and optimize the benefits of a search engine. It could also get expensive.

Signs: "We buy houses for ca$h!!" You have probably seen these signs on the side of the road while waiting at a stop light. Although they may work, they appear cheap and may not be welcome in the neighborhood. Alternatively, you can "wrap" your car or place a magnetic sign on your car.

To sum up Commandment 5, wholesaling is a very active way of getting into real estate—where you stop wholesaling, you stop generating income. If you love it and enjoy the process, keep using wholesale as your main strategy. At the same time, you can hustle and wholesale to raise capital to invest in your real estate education, and make your capital work passively for you through different strategies. Be persistent, be creative with your marketing strategies, know what buyers are looking for, and be ready for the opportunities.

From the book, *The Compound Effect*, by Darren Hardy:

Preparation (personal growth) + Attitude (belief/mindset) + Opportunity (a good thing coming your way) + Action (doing something about it) = LUCK

Exercise:

Where can you find wholesale deals?

_____

Do these deals meet the criteria? Is there anything you can do creatively to make this deal work?

- ALWAYS make money in the buy.
- Leave something on the table for the next person.
- Make it a WIN-WIN: provide solutions to problems. The bigger the problem, the greater the profit.

_____

Commandment 6

Private Lending

As mentioned, the simple definition of "financial freedom" is to have enough passive income to cover your expenses. I have a sticker on my computer that says, "If your money isn't working for you, then you will never stop working for money." When my kids use my computer, they always see the sticker. They know this line by heart as a good reminder for us to make money work for us. This is what leveraging is about. Imagine what your life would be like if you could make money while you sleep, and not have to trade your precious time for money.

> *"If you don't find a way to make money while you sleep,*
> *you will work till you die."*
> **~ Warren Buffet**

The purpose of this section is to show you how to "be the bank," and what your options are when the banks say no. I wish I had started doing private lending sooner in my real estate career. However, I have no regrets knowing more about different strategies and what my funds would be used for before I started lending money out as a private lender. On the other hand, if you are a flipper, or if you have different projects on the go that require quick access to money and flexible terms, private money is a very powerful way to scale your real estate business.

Different Financing Options

As an investor, you may reach a point where you have leveraged so much of your mortgageability that you can no longer qualify or borrow from institutional lenders. That is a good problem to have. That means you are actively investing and understand the power of leveraging. Nevertheless, major banks, or what we often refer to as A-lenders, are not the only source of financing. There are different financing options available to you. This is where great mortgage brokers on your power team can help to strategize and maximize the return in your portfolio.

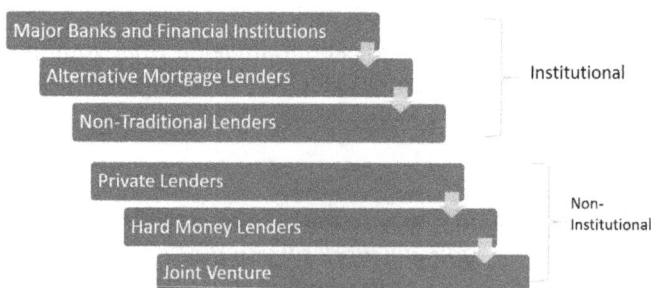

Major Banks and Financial Institutions
Alternative Mortgage Lenders
Non-Traditional Lenders

Institutional

Private Lenders
Hard Money Lenders
Joint Venture

Non-Institutional

Major banks and financial institutions usually provide loans at the best rates and terms. The lenders have a strict rule and criteria that they follow. They focus on both the property and the borrower's qualifications in terms of credit, proof of income, debt ratios, and down payment. They will also look at the condition of the property. If it is not livable (e.g., roof, mold, and foundation problems that require major repair), banks and major institutions may require a remedy or holdback until the issues are addressed.

Alternative mortgage lenders, such as credit unions and monoline lenders, can provide you with the best rates and terms, just like the major banks and financial institutions. They may be more flexible on calculating your debt ratios and the number of properties you may have.

Non-traditional lenders are alternative trust companies and other approved lenders that are more flexible with incomes when qualifying a mortgage, but at a higher interest rate. If you are self-employed with a lower taxable income, or you have a lower credit score, this could be an option for you. However, lenders usually require the property to be located in a good area and be in a liveable condition.

That is all the real estate in this section that I will devote to institutional lending options. Our focus in this section is on non-institutional lending options. For the purpose of this book, or from my personal experience, I consider hard money as a type of private lending. I have seen mortgage brokers or other investors define hard money as short-term and high-interest loans from individuals, whereas the private money could come from personal RRSPs, companies with funds to lend, or friends and family.

Lending Criteria

I love private lending, because it is so simple. Basically, you just need to know the following criteria:

1. **How much?**
2. **How long?**
3. **What is the security?**
4. **What is the return?**
5. **"Trust"**

1. **How much?** It really depends on how much you have available to lend out. I have loaned as little as $20,000 to help a flipper complete a yard and put finishing touches to improve the curb appeal of a property before putting it on the market.

2. **How long?** If you have money sitting idle short term, waiting for the next investment property to come on the market, lend the money out, short term, to other investors to make your money work for you. You can do a short-term loan for a few months to under a year.

    As the borrower, the interest rates may seem high to you. If you are borrowing $100,000 at 12% for 6 months, you are paying $6000 to have access to the funds in order to complete a $100,000 renovation project, so why not?

3. **What is the security?** The most secure thing to do is to put your money in a GIC at a bank, with 1% interest rate as your return. However, it is a sure loss, as the inflation is normally more than 1%. Your wealth is shrinking in this case.

    As trained real estate investors, we are investing with control, and we are in this to make money. It is "usually" secured against real estate as collateral. Notice the word "usually." Trucks, boats, or other objects of value could also be collateral. LTV (loan to value) is another important factor to consider when evaluating how secure it is. LTV is the ratio of the debt vs. the appraised value of the property. When banks require you to have a 20% down payment, they are lending at 80% LTV. The 20% is basically the bank's security, meaning that the bank's loan is secured as long as the housing price does not drop more than 20%.

4. **What is the return?** We are in this to make money and receive a good ROI, as in any real estate investment. Think like the bank. The return depends on the security or the risk, as we just discussed. It also depends on the experience of the lenders and the borrowers. An experienced flipper, for example, will more likely get loans with better terms, since they know what they are doing, and they have a record of repayments. On the other hand, as seasoned investors or lenders, we know the return we are looking for, and we have the network to find good lending opportunities to

make money work for us. Hard money lenders may be looking at 12%–15% annual return, with 1%–2% lender fees.

5. **Trust:** In addition to these criteria, it all comes down to "trust." You have to know, like, and trust the people you lend money to. You can go through mortgage brokers that you trust to find private lending opportunities, as well as your own network. I prefer to find lending opportunities in my own network. It is also a good way to build relationships with other investors and get involved in various projects. For example, I am not handy. There are other people who are talented and amazing at staging, designing, and renovating major projects. I could learn from them, and be part of it by providing funds or sharing equity with my partners. Again, your network is your net worth. There are also flippers that have tried to refer tenant buyers to me. We are helping each other grow our businesses and create more win-win opportunities.

Advantages of Private Lending

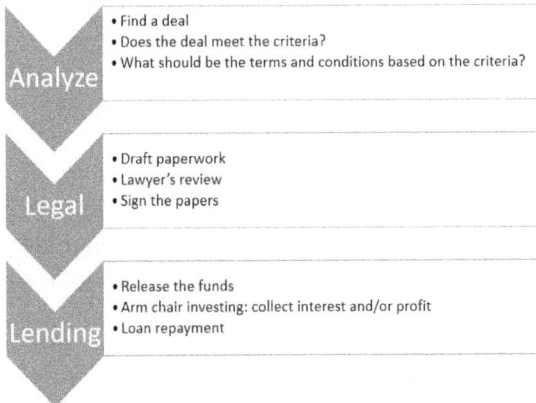

Analyze
- Find a deal
- Does the deal meet the criteria?
- What should be the terms and conditions based on the criteria?

Legal
- Draft paperwork
- Lawyer's review
- Sign the papers

Lending
- Release the funds
- Arm chair investing: collect interest and/or profit
- Loan repayment

This chart summarizes the lending process. It is pretty simple and straightforward. If you have a busy life, trying to juggle kids' activities, work, and your social life, the biggest advantage of private lending is that it is simple and does not require a lot of time. Time is everything when you have a busy life and are aiming to scale your business. I have included a few samples of loan agreements just to illustrate how simple it could be. It could be as simple as a two-page contract. Regardless, please consult your lawyer for legal advice.

Additionally, it is flexible. You can decide the terms and how much risk you are willing to take. Solid financial literacy will help you understand the risks and how your money is secured against hard assets. As the borrower, you can evaluate if the terms, flexibility, and cost of borrowing is worth it to you. If not, you might want to consider if you have a good deal to attract the money with the terms you need.

The Power of Leveraging

Here is an important concept to remember about leveraging: good debt vs. bad debt. ***Good debt puts money in your pocket***. Only borrow money when you can make money work for you.

Home Worth	$1,500,000	
80% Loan to Value	$1,200,000	
Owes	$ 600,000	
HELOC	$600,000	

Scenario: $600K at 12%, 1% lender fee		
Monthly Revenue:	$6,000	
HELOC Interest	$1,475	Simple Interest 2.95% (Prime + 0.5%)
Monthly Mortgage $	2,530	Assuming Mortgage at 3%, 30 yr term
Monthly Cash flow	$1,995	

Annual cash flow		
Cash Flow		$23,940
Lender Fee	$	6,000
Total:		$29,940

Let me paint you a picture and show you how you can live in your house mortgage-free, and potentially get some cash flow. I also find that it is a good tool to show investors how to leverage the equity in their homes.

Let's assume that your home is worth $1,500,000, and you still have $600,000 of mortgage on it. If you refinance and get 80% loan to value—so $1,200,000, out of the property—you can get $600,000 of HELOC at your disposal. HELOC stands for "Home Equity Line of Credit," secured against your home. It could be a flexible, low-interest funding solution, and could be your emergency source of capital when you need it.

In this case, we are assuming that you have a monthly mortgage payment of $2,530. (I rounded off the numbers; in case the analytical bug in you is wondering why it is not precise to the second dismal place.) If you take out $600,000 from a HELOC, and make 12% interest, then that means you will be able to make $6,000 in interest per month, passively. After paying your mortgage, you can have close to $2,000 in cash flow. Hey, you could even have your utilities covered.

On top of the interest earnings, there often is a lender fee, regardless of the loan period. In this example, I am using a 1% lender fee. In total, you can make close to $30,000 passively. It is like having somebody in the household working part time to have some extra income. I have two young kids at home. It will be nice, one day, when they can start contributing. In the meantime, make your money work harder for you.

Funds Available:

From My Investor	$	150,000
Scenario: A Lending Opportunity $150,000 at 12%		
Monthly Revenue	$	1,500
Interest Paid to My investor 6%	$	750
Montly Cash Flow	$	750

Your network is your net worth. It gets easier as you build your network and are more familiar with how the moving parts work in a deal. Since we have just gone through the section on wholesaling, here is another example I would like to share with you, to show you how simple it could be using a hybrid strategy of wholesaling and private lending. I have an investor with $150,000 in capital. We have known each other for more than 20 years. He is not interested in learning to be a working partner in a real estate deal. He wants something simple and secure. I happened to have an investor/flipper approaching me with an opportunity requiring $150,000 Canadian in capital, at 12% return. I offered my investor a fixed 6% return guaranteed. As Suze Omen always says, "People first, then money, then things." I want to make sure my relationship with my family, friends, and investors come before money. They get what they are looking for, and I make a passive income of $750 a month. It is a win-win for everybody.

Joint Ventures (JV)

Joint ventures is about one plus one being greater than 2. It is about leveraging your resources with those of others. We are problem solvers as real estate investors. If you are lacking knowledge and time to execute, leveraging other people's time and resources is a smart way to scale. Having joint venture partners is how I was able to scale and reach my goal of financial freedom the "royal way." I have been the money partner and I have been the working partner in most of my deals. Choose your partners carefully! People are more important than money. It is not worth the worries and sleepless nights, even if you make money in a real estate deal. In contrast, it is very rewarding when you work toward the same goals and help each other grow in a great partnership.

Fifty percent of something is better than 100% of nothing. The most common joint ventures are 50/50 partnerships. As you are more experienced and financially literate, you can actually get creative in structuring your deals. The same concepts we pointed out earlier still apply: Always leave money for your JVs in the deal. Be fair; it has to be a win-win, or it is not a deal.

A joint venture agreement does not have to be complicated. These are the main points in a typical joint venture agreement, and some examples:

Purpose of the Joint Venture Agreement

The purpose of this agreement is to identify the understanding of the 50/50 split between _____ and _____ regarding the property: (address here)

Roles and Responsibilities

- *Responsibilities of (name or company of the working partner)*
- *Tenant placement*

- *Managing and coordinating with all necessary parties, such as realtors, lawyers, mortgage brokers, insurance brokers, etc.*
- *Responsibilities of (name or company of the investor)*
- *Keeping a dedicated bank account*
- *Arranging financing*
- *Promptly forwarding copies of any correspondence he/she receives regarding property tax, etc.*

Compensation

Cash flow will be distributed 50/50 to the working partner and investor after all expenses are paid.

Percentage of Interest

50/50 split

Cash Calls

Each party agrees to cover 50% of cash shortfalls.

Proceeds of Sales

Following disposition of the property, the investor shall be entitled to receive the amount paid for the down payment, as well as all expenses and other payments paid by the investor pursuant to the Joint Venture Agreement, as well as any fees associated with the purchase of the property.

Death of Either Party

The death of either party shall not act to terminate the joint venture. The estate of the deceased joint venturer shall continue as a member thereof, and shall share in any future profits or loss as here above provided.

This was the very first deal I had when I started to get real estate education. It was a small deal and my first step of taking action. It was a single-family home in Windsor, Ontario. I have never even seen the property, and I already sold it earlier this year. Something I learned from my first real estate class was to "stop looking at properties." In addition, we do not necessarily have to invest in our backyard. To scale your real estate portfolio, remember to look for ways to free up your time and other resources as well.

Leverage Other People's Money (OPM); Leverage Other People's Time (OPT)

It was the first joint venture for both my managing partner and me. We were sitting at the same round table in an "Income Property" class. It is easier to do business with people who were educated in the same way and have the same mindset. We are action takers. He mentioned that he had the connections and an idea of getting single-family homes to rent to Syrian refugees. The rent was guaranteed, and we would have tenants right away with no vacancies.

I leveraged his time, and he leveraged my ability to come in the deal with the down payment and mortgage. It was a 50/50 joint venture, meaning that all the cash flow and expenses are split 50/50. Here is a summary of our responsibilities:

Example: 50/50 SFH

Investors: Brooke
- Down payment & closing cost
- On title & mortgage
- Renovation cost $5000
- Signed JV agreement
- Cover 50% cash flow or calls
- Independent legal advise
- Sign JV agreement

Managing Partner:
- Power team
- Skills: renovate, converting 3-4 bedroom
- Local expertise: Guarantee 0 vacancy
- Cover 50% cash flow or calls
- Manage property
- Sign JV agreement
- o Exit Strategy: First right of refusal: Brooke will sell the property to managing partner at 3% annual appreciation

Here are the numbers: The purchase price of the property was $113,000. I used my HELOC (home equity line of credit) for the down payment and closing cost. Therefore, besides the mortgage of 80% LTV (loan to value), I was leveraging the bank's money for the down payment, closing cost, and renovation cost of $5,000. With $5000, we were able to convert the three-bedroom house into a four-bedroom house, because we leveraged my partner's local connections.

We used a hybrid strategy, where my managing partner would have the first right of refusal to have the option to buy the property at the end of JV at an agreed price. Option contracts are usually used in the investment strategy known as rent to own or lease option, where the option contract states what the buy-back price is on a specific date if he chooses to buy the property. Rent to own is the strategy I focus on that enables me to generate amazing cash flow and return on investment. I will devote a section later in this book to discuss how "rent to own" works.

We calculated the option price based on 20% of return for me as the investor. My partner and I were able to receive an average of $200 cash flow each, after the mortgage and all expenses are paid. It does not seem like a lot. However, I only put in an initial investment of $28,800. On top of that, the $28,800 came from my HELOC (home equity line of credit). This means that I was again leveraging the bank's money. I did not put in any of my hard-working earned or saved money. The cash flow of $200 is after my HELOC interest is paid.

This property was in Windsor. It is crazy to think that at the time I purchased the property, I was actually advised against buying a property in Windsor, because the market had not done so well in prior years. As investors, we are not depending on appreciation alone to create wealth if we want to create a viable real estate business and expand our portfolio. In this case, for example, even if there is no appreciation, I used none of my own money, and I generated $200 of cash flow per month.

- Purchase price: $113,000
- Renovation: $5,000
- Down payment and Closing: $23,800
- Monthly CF: $200 for investor
- Initial investment: $23,800+$5,000= $28,800
- Option Price: **$128,900**

- Cash flow: $7,200
- Appreciation: $10,900
- Mortgage pay down: $5,045
  - final repair cost: $3,500
  - Closing cost: $2,000
- Profit: $17,645
- ROI: $24.42%

I have taken action. However, with the example of my first deal, you can see that it would take me a very long time, at $200 per door, to have enough cash flow to replace my income. I set a goal of making $100,000 the first year. Back then, I do not think that I really believed that the goal would be achievable, because I had a busy life planned that year. I had two major trips planned, work, and no clear action plan. In the second year, I changed my goal to have enough cash flow to replace my working income. That was how I was able to reach my financial goal in three years.

After going through different strategies and examples, you can see that we can combine different strategies, doing a hybrid and being creative using real estate as a tool. I have combined the wholesaling and lease option strategies. I have also used wholesaling, the idea of leveraging OPM, and flipping, in the previous example. Nonetheless, there are more moving parts to each strategy. The content provided in this book is a good starting point to get information and learn about different strategies. There are books devoted on each strategy. I highly encourage you to explore more on the strategies you want to focus on. More importantly, I recommend that you get advanced training and hire a mentor so that you know how to apply these strategies correctly, legally, and ethically.

Exercise:

List your current sources of funding, including your own and OPM (other people's money).

Savings

_____

Credit limits (e.g., lines of credit, credit cards)

_____

Equity in property (e.g., HELOC)

_____

RRSP, LIRA, RESP, TSFA, etc.

_____

Your network (e.g., friends and family, private sources)

_____

Commandment 7

Conclusion

The aim of this book is to inspire you to get started in learning about real estate investing, and to apply the knowledge by taking massive action to be a successful real estate investor. The biggest obstacle that holds people back is the self-doubt and fear of failure. That is why it is so important to have the network that supports you, and to have a big enough goal to give you the drive to get over self-doubt, not get discouraged, and have the stamina to persist. I have gone through a corporate career and traditional schooling all the way to graduate school. Compared to calculus, management accounting, and learning about company policies or SOPs, the concept of real estate strategies is really not that hard at all. Overcoming limiting beliefs, and transforming our old selves, is the hardest part.

I have seen a lot of real estate investor "wannabes" waiting on the sidelines to get into real estate investing. Here is a good quote: *"If you play not to lose, you will never win."* **All those people waiting for a market correction in order to buy an investment property are still waiting**. Besides, why would you even bother wasting your time being in the game if that is the case, and what is the fun in that? Getting educated and being a seasoned investor is about control and increasing your chance of winning.

The best way of compressing your time to be financially free in a "royal way," is to have a mentor accelerate your path to success with his or her experience and expertise. Even the best of the best in the world continue to hire coaches and mentors. You do not need to reinvent the wheel. Find a mentor that can point out obstacles in your path, save you time, and push you to be uncomfortable. At the same time, you must respect and cherish your mentor's time and resources. Don't be cheap on hiring a good coach or mentor. Be prepared to do the work. You can focus on one or two strategies first. Your mentor will give you clarity when you are overwhelmed or off track. Somebody did it for me, and I wish to pay it forward to help more people create health through real estate, through this book and other media. This quote from Zig Ziglar resonates with me: *"You can have everything in life you want, if you will just help other people get what they want."*

Ten months ago, when I decided to write this book, I had absolutely no idea what I was going to put in the book. With all the deals I have done, I had no clue how to formulate the ideas in order to offer the audience something valuable and worth their time reading.

Luckily, the Universe has its own magic way of making things happen and opening doors of opportunities for us. I remember going on my first speaking engagement of more than 150 people. I announced that I was the author of this upcoming book, when I only had a page of introduction, and the table of contents were not even ready. Somehow, I believed, and I just knew that I would get this book done. Set an intention, and let the rest happen for you.

"Whatever the mind can conceive and believe, it can achieve."
~ **Napoleon Hill**

I am merely one of many real estate investors who have done it, as proof to you that it can be done and it has been achieved. It is then much easier for your mind to conceive, believe, and lead you to achieve.

"Your legacy is every life you have touched."
~ **Oprah Winfrey**

I hope this book has inspired you and touched your life in a positive way. Ultimately, it is up to you to maximize the reality of your situation and everything that is about to happen to you. The most rewarding thing is to witness your own transformation in your pursuit to financial freedom. I cannot wait to hear about the legacy you have created, and about your transformation in your pursuit to financial freedom the "royal way."

Take massive action. Happy investing!!

About the Author

From a stay-at-home mom of 10 years, to being financially free in 3 years, Brooke's journey as a real estate entrepreneur is one that is inspirational and, more importantly, duplicable. Shortly after returning to the corporate world, Brooke also began to pursue financial education. Having been inspired by books like *Rich Dad, Poor Dad*, she chose to leverage real estate investing strategies to create multiple streams of income. Since 2016, lease option (commonly known as rent to own) has been a main, focused strategy for her. To date, in addition to a number of lease options that she has executed, Brooke has also completed several duplex conversions, private lending deals, and has invested in land development projects. This has enabled her to replace her corporate income with the cash flow from her portfolio, while learning, networking, and traveling with her family. Brooke is now a coach in real estate investing. She believes that she will be able help others create the results they want, with the proper training and guidance —the same way she was coached and mentored.

Brooke has an MBA from Schulich School of Business, at York University, and a Hons BA from the University of Toronto, in Economics and Environmental Studies. Currently, she continues to work as a management consultant while expanding her real estate portfolio. Her goal is to be financially free on her own terms. However, she knows that she loves helping others create wealth through real estate, too much to ever quit.

The author is available for coaching and delivering keynote presentations to appropriate audiences. For rates and availability, please contact the author directly.

www.ingramcontent.com/pod-product-compliance
Lightning Source LLC
Chambersburg PA
CBHW070407200326
41518CB00011B/2100